Bro

Oxford
Junior
Thesaurus

Compiled by: Sheila Dignen

OXFORD
UNIVERSITY PRESS

OXFORD

UNIVERSITY PRESS

Great Clarendon Street, Oxford OX2 6DP

Oxford University Press is a department of the University of Oxford.
It furthers the University's objective of excellence in research, scholarship,
and education by publishing worldwide in

Oxford New York

Auckland Bangkok Buenos Aires Cape Town Chennai
Dar es Salaam Delhi Hong Kong Istanbul Karachi Kolkata
Kuala Lumpur Madrid Melbourne Mexico City Mumbai Nairobi
São Paulo Singapore Taipei Tokyo Toronto

Oxford is a registered trade mark of Oxford University Press
in the UK and in certain other countries

British Library cataloguing in Publication Data available

ISBN 0-19-910857-9

10 9 8 7 6 5 4 3

Printed in Italy by G. Canale & C. S.p.A.

Do you have a query about words, their origin, meaning, use, spelling,
pronunciation, or any other aspect of the English language? Visit our
website at www.askoxford.com where you will be able to find answers
to your language queries.

Preface for teachers and parents

This new edition of the *Oxford Junior Thesaurus* is up to date with revised vocabulary, panels and supplementary usage and grammar notes in the endmatter. It uses a straightforward approach to help primary school children build and enrich their vocabulary and master the skills of using a thesaurus. It is particularly useful for 6-8 year olds and, in the UK, it fulfils the National Literacy Strategy requirements for YR2 - YR4 and Scottish Guidelines P3, 4, and 5.

The headwords have all been carefully chosen as words that children are most likely to look up. The alternative words offered are a mixture of familiar words and unfamiliar words that will stretch and develop children's vocabulary. For example, the entry **disappointed** lists the synonyms **upset** and **sad**, which will be familiar to children, and also **dejected** and **downcast**, which may be new to them. Particular attention has been given to overused words such as **big, go, good, nice,** and **say**, to encourage children to experiment with alternatives.

The headwords in this thesaurus are arranged alphabetically. Where a headword has several different meanings or uses, an example sentence is given to distinguish meaning.

There are two main types of entry. There are entries that give synonyms or words that are very close in meaning to the headword. These are listed after the headword and example sentence. All the words listed after an example sentence can replace the headword in the sentence without changing the meaning. Where a synonym has a slightly different meaning to the headword, a note is given explaining this difference. For example, at the headword **laugh**, the synonym **guffaw** is listed with the explanation (*to laugh very loudly*). Where it is felt that children need help with using a synonym, for example if its grammar is not the same as the grammar of the headword, an example sentence is also included. For example, at the entry for **frighten** the phrase **to give someone a fright** is given and is illustrated with its own example to show how it should be used in a sentence. With some words, it is difficult to find a useful synonym for children when the word is taken in isolation. An example is the verb **forget**, where in a typical sentence such as *I've forgotten his name*, there are no direct synonyms of the headword. In these cases, alternative ways of expressing a whole sentence are included, for example *I can't remember it. It has slipped my mind.*

There are other entries that give related words rather than synonyms. For example, at the entry for **dog**, some types of dog are included, for example **Alsatian, boxer,** and **collie**, and also related words such as **bark, yap, growl** and **snarl**. These entries will be useful for children looking for more precise words in a general subject area.

This thesaurus forms an excellent companion volume to the *Oxford Junior Dictionary*. It is already a favourite with children and this new edition will be an invaluable tool both in the classroom and at home.

Sheila Dignen

Using this thesaurus

A thesaurus helps you choose just the right word for what you want to say or write. It lists the words that you are most likely to look up and gives alternatives for them. These are called *synonyms*. Using words that are more accurate and varied will make your writing more interesting.

A special focus is given to words that are often overused, for example, *big* and *nice*. There are also entries that give a range of vocabulary that you may use when writing about a particular topic for example, *aeroplane* or *rain*. Then there are entries giving lists of examples of the headword, for example, *bird* and *tree*.

You will also find example sentences to help with context and opposites, or *antonyms*.

In this thesaurus you will find:

Headwords

The headwords are the words in the thesaurus that you look up. They are in alphabetical order and are printed in colour so that you can find them easily.

Alphabet with virtual thumb tabs

The alphabet down the side of the page helps you to navigate your way around the thesaurus.

Example sentences

The example sentences show the different meanings of the headword, so that you can find the exact meaning you are looking for.

Synonyms

The synonyms are the words that mean the same as the headword. You can use one of the synonyms instead of the word you are looking up.

Antonyms

Antonyms are the opposite of the synonyms. Knowing these helps you to grasp the exact meaning of the word and builds your vocabulary.

Example of a synonym

Sometimes an example sentence is given to show you exactly how you should use the synonym in a sentence.

Phrase with synonym

Some words do not have many synonyms, so sometimes we include a whole phrase which gives you another way of expressing the meaning of the headword.

Labels

You will find labels giving information about the synonyms if their meaning is not exactly the same as that of the headword. The labels will help you to understand the difference in meaning.

Panels

Throughout the thesaurus, you will find panels that give you extra words. There are panels that give alternative sentences using the headword, there are panels giving examples of the headword and there are panels that give a whole range of words that you may use to describe the headword.

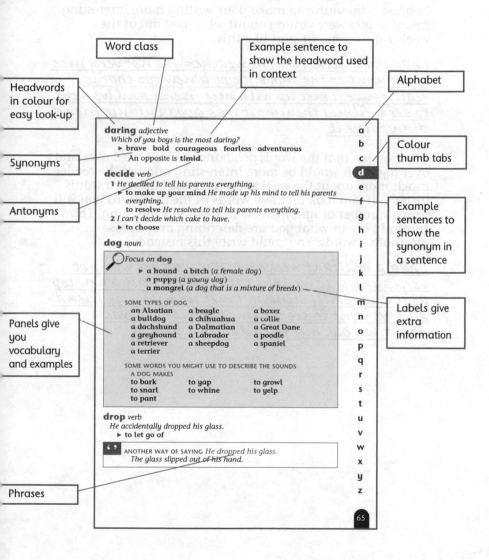

Thesaurus Features

Word class

Example sentence to show the headword used in context

Alphabet

Headwords in colour for easy look-up

Colour thumb tabs

Synonyms

Antonyms

Example sentences to show the synonym in a sentence

Panels give you vocabulary and examples

Labels give extra information

Phrases

---

daring *adjective*
Which of you boys is the most daring?
► **brave bold courageous fearless adventurous**
An opposite is **timid**.

decide *verb*
1 *He decided to tell his parents everything.*
► **to make up your mind** *He made up his mind to tell his parents everything.*
to resolve *He resolved to tell his parents everything.*
2 *I can't decide which cake to have.*
► **to choose**

dog *noun*

Focus on **dog**
► **a hound a bitch** (*a female dog*)
a puppy (*a young dog*)
a mongrel (*a dog that is a mixture of breeds*)

SOME TYPES OF DOG

an Alsatian	a beagle	a boxer
a bulldog	a chihuahua	a collie
a dachshund	a Dalmatian	a Great Dane
a greyhound	a Labrador	a poodle
a retriever	a sheepdog	a spaniel
a terrier		

SOME WORDS YOU MIGHT USE TO DESCRIBE THE SOUNDS
A DOG MAKES

to bark	to yap	to growl
to snarl	to whine	to yelp
to pant		

drop *verb*
He accidentally dropped his glass.
► **to let go of**

" ANOTHER WAY OF SAYING *He dropped his glass.*
The glass slipped out of his hand.

a
b
c
d
e
f
g
h
i
j
k
l
m
n
o
p
q
r
s
t
u
v
w
x
y
z

Making your writing more interesting

You use a thesaurus to make your writing more interesting. Imagine you were writing about what you did at the weekend. You might start like this:

I had good weekend. The weather was not very nice so we went to the shops. I got a new top that is really nice. I met up with my friend and we went to see a film. I thought it was good but my friend didn't like it.

Can you see that the words *good* and *nice* are used over and over again? It would be more interesting and tell the reader much more about the weekend if you used different words instead. If you look up these words in the thesaurus you will find a number of synonyms with a similar meaning. Think carefully about what you are describing and choose alternative words. You could write this instead:

I had a brilliant weekend. The weather was not very sunny so we went to the shops. I got a new top and it is really stylish. I met up with my friend and we went to see a film. I thought it was amusing but my friend didn't like it.

ability *noun*

1 *You have the ability to do very well at school.*
  ▶ **capability   intelligence**

2 *He's a young footballer with a lot of ability.*
  ▶ **talent   skill   flair**

about *adverb*

There are about thirty children in our class.
  ▶ **roughly   approximately**

absolutely *adverb*

We got absolutely soaked!
  ▶ **completely   totally   utterly**

accept *verb*

The children stepped forward to accept their prizes.
  ▶ **to take   to receive**
  ← → An opposite is **reject**.

accident *noun*

1 *There was an accident on the motorway.*
  ▶ **a crash   a smash   a collision**
    a pile-up (*an accident with a lot of cars*)

2 *I'm sorry, it was an accident.*
  ▶ **a mistake**

> 💬 **OTHER WAYS OF SAYING** *It was an accident.*
> *It was accidental.*
> *I did it accidentally.*
> *I didn't mean to do it.*
> *It wasn't deliberate.*
> *I didn't do it on purpose.*

accidentally *adverb*

I accidentally knocked the lamp over.
  ▶ **unintentionally   inadvertently**
  ← → An opposite is **deliberately**.

a
b
c
d
e
f
g
h
i
j
k
l
m
n
o
p
q
r
s
t
u
v
w
x
y
z

a
b
c
d
e
f
g
h
i
j
k
l
m
n
o
p
q
r
s
t
u
v
w
x
y
z

accurate *adjective*
She gave the police an accurate description of the thief.
▶ exact precise correct
←→ An opposite is **inaccurate**.

achieve *verb*
You have achieved a lot this term.
▶ to do to accomplish

achievement *noun*
Winning a gold medal is a great achievement.
▶ an accomplishment a feat a success

act *verb*
1 We must act quickly to save these animals.
▶ to do something to take action
2 I would love to act on the stage.
▶ to perform to appear

action *noun*
1 I like films that are full of action.
▶ excitement suspense
2 His brave action saved his sister's life.
▶ an act a deed

active *adjective*
Most children enjoy being active.
▶ busy lively energetic on the go
←→ An opposite is **inactive**.

activity *noun*
What activities do you do outside school?
▶ a hobby a pastime an interest

actual *adjective*
This is the actual ship that Nelson sailed on.
▶ real genuine very

add *verb*
Mix the butter and sugar together, then add the eggs.
▶ to mix in

admire *verb*
1 Which sports stars do you admire?
▶ to respect   to look up to   to idolize   to hero-worship
2 We stood and admired the lovely view.
▶ to enjoy   to appreciate

admit *verb*
He admitted that he had broken the window.
▶ to confess   to own up
← → An opposite is **deny**.

adult *noun*
You must be accompanied by an adult.
▶ a grown-up

advantage *noun*
Being tall is an advantage in some sports.
▶ a help   an asset
← → An opposite is **disadvantage**.

adventure *noun*
He told us about all his exciting adventures.
▶ an escapade   an exploit

advertise *verb*
We made some posters to advertise the jumble sale.
▶ to publicize   to promote

advice *noun*
He gave me some very useful advice.
▶ help   guidance
   a suggestion He made a useful suggestion.

a
b
c
d
e
f
g
h
i
j
k
l
m
n
o
p
q
r
s
t
u
v
w
x
y
z

a
b
c
d
e
f
g
h
i
j
k
l
m
n
o
p
q
r
s
t
u
v
w
x
y
z

aeroplane noun

Focus on **aeroplane**

He had never been in an aeroplane before.
► **a plane   an aircraft**

SOME TYPES OF AEROPLANE
an airliner   a fighter plane   a glider
a jet   a jumbo jet

SOME WORDS YOU MIGHT USE TO DESCRIBE HOW AN
AEROPLANE FLIES
to fly   to glide   to hover
to zoom   to dive   to take off
to land

afraid adjective

1 *Are you afraid of spiders?*
► **frightened   scared   terrified** (*very frightened*)

2 *I was afraid the boat might capsize.*
► **worried   nervous   fearful**

aggressive adjective

1 *Tigers are very aggressive animals.*
► **fierce**

2 *You shouldn't be so aggressive with your brother.*
► **rough   violent**

←→ An opposite is **friendly**.

agree verb

I agree with you.
► **to be of the same opinion as someone** *I am of the same opinion as you.*
to share someone's view *I share your view.*

←→ An opposite is **disagree**.

aim verb

He aimed his bike at the ramp.
► **to point**

alarm noun
The fire alarm went off.
▶ a signal   a siren

alert adjective
The sentries on duty must remain alert.
▶ ready   awake   on the lookout

alive adjective
The bird was injured but still alive.
▶ living   breathing
← → An opposite is **dead**.

allow verb
They allowed us to use their swimming pool.
▶ to let *They let us use their swimming pool.*
   to permit *They permitted us to use the swimming pool.*
   to give someone permission *They gave us permission to use the swimming pool.*
← → An opposite is **forbid**.

all right adjective
1 *Are you all right?*
▶ well   safe   unhurt   healthy
2 *The food was all right, but not brilliant.*
▶ OK   acceptable   satisfactory

almost adverb
I've almost finished.
▶ nearly   virtually   practically

amaze verb
He amazed us with his magic tricks.
▶ to astonish   to astound

amazed adjective
I was amazed when I saw his new bike.
▶ astonished   staggered   flabbergasted (*informal*)   stunned

amazing *adjective*
What an amazing car!
▶ **wonderful fantastic incredible phenomenal**

ambition *noun*
Her ambition is to be a doctor.
▶ **a dream a goal an aim a wish**

amount *noun*
They ate a huge amount of food!
▶ **a quantity**

amuse *verb*
His jokes amused us all.
▶ **to entertain to make someone laugh**

amusing *adjective*
He told us a very amusing story.
▶ **funny humorous entertaining**

anger *noun*
She couldn't hide her anger.
▶ **annoyance**
irritation (*slight anger*)
fury (*great anger*)
rage (*great anger*)

angry *adjective*
Mum looked very angry.
▶ **cross annoyed**
irritated (*slightly angry*)
furious (*very angry*)
livid (*very angry indeed*)
←→ An opposite is **calm**.

> 99
> OTHER WAYS OF SAYING *She became angry.*
> *She lost her temper.*
> *She flew off the handle.*

animal *noun*
What sort of animal was it?
▶ a creature   a beast (*a fierce animal*)

••• SOME TYPES OF ANIMAL
a mammal   a bird   a fish
a reptile   an amphibian   an insect

SOME FARM ANIMALS
chicken   cow   duck
goose   horse   pig
sheep

SOME ANIMALS THAT ARE POPULAR AS PETS
cat   dog   gerbil
guinea pig   hamster   pony
rabbit   tropical fish

SOME WILD ANIMALS YOU MIGHT SEE IN BRITAIN
badger   fox   hare
hedgehog   mole   mouse
rabbit   rat   squirrel

SOME WILD ANIMALS FROM HOT COUNTRIES
baboon   camel   cheetah
chimpanzee   crocodile   deer
elephant   gazelle   giraffe
gorilla   hippopotamus leopard
lion   monkey   panther
penguin   rhinoceros   tiger
zebra

SOME WILD ANIMALS FROM COLD COUNTRIES
penguin   polar bear   reindeer
wolf

SOME WILD ANIMALS FROM AUSTRALIA
kangaroo   koala   kookaburra
wallaby   wombat

SOME WILD ANIMALS THAT LIVE IN THE SEA
dolphin   fish   octopus
seal   sea-lion   shark
turtle   walrus   whale

a b c d e f g h i j k l m n o p q r s t u v w x y z

a
b
c
d
e
f
g
h
i
j
k
l
m
n
o
p
q
r
s
t
u
v
w
x
y
z

annoy *verb*

1 *The loud music was annoying me.*
▶ to irritate
to get on someone's nerves *The loud music was getting on my nerves.*
2 *My little brother keeps annoying me!*
▶ to pester to bother to tease to bug
←→ An opposite is **please**.

annoyed *adjective*
My mum was quite annoyed with me.
▶ cross angry irritated exasperated
←→ An opposite is **pleased**.

annoying *adjective*
Sometimes my sister can be very annoying.
▶ irritating tiresome

answer *noun*
I called his name, but there was no answer.
▶ a reply a response

answer *verb*
I shouted to her, but she didn't answer.
▶ to reply to respond

apologize *verb*
I apologized for being rude.
▶ to say sorry

appear *verb*
The ship appeared on the horizon.
▶ to arrive to come into view to become visible
←→ An opposite is **disappear**.

appetite *noun*
I lost my appetite when I was ill.
▶ hunger desire for food

appointment *noun*
Your appointment is at two o'clock.
▶ a meeting an interview

approach *verb*
I started to feel nervous as we approached the theatre.
▶ to come near to   to come towards

appropriate *adjective*
Those clothes are not appropriate for a disco.
▶ suitable   acceptable   right

area *noun*
1 *There is a special area where you can play.*
▶ a place   a space   a patch
2 *This is a very nice area of the city.*
▶ a part   a district

argue *verb*
Why are you two always arguing?
▶ to quarrel   to squabble   to fight   to fall out   to bicker
to disagree
← → An opposite is **agree**.

argument *noun*
They had a big argument.
▶ a quarrel   a disagreement   a row   a fight

arrange *verb*
1 *She arranged the books carefully on the shelf.*
▶ to place   to set out
2 *We have arranged to meet at ten o'clock.*
▶ to plan   to agree
3 *My mother has arranged everything for my party.*
▶ to organize   to plan

arrest *verb*
The police have arrested the robbers.
▶ to catch   to capture
to take prisoner *The police have taken the robbers prisoner.*
to take into custody *The police have taken the robbers into custody.*

arrive *verb*

1 *We finally arrived in London.*
▶ to reach   to get to

2 *Jessica arrived at the party two hours late.*
▶ to come   to turn up

3 *When does the plane arrive in New York?*
▶ to land   to touch down   to get in

4 *The boat should arrive at ten o'clock.*
▶ to land   to dock   to get in

← → An opposite is **depart**.

art *noun*

I really enjoy doing art at school.
▶ drawing   painting   sketching   modelling   pottery
  sculpture   graphics

ashamed *adjective*

He was ashamed of what he had done.
▶ **sorry** *He was sorry for what he had done.*
  upset *He was upset about what he had done.*
  remorseful *He was remorseful for what he had done.*

ask *verb*

He asked me what my name was.
▶ to enquire

ask for *verb*

1 *I've asked for a new bike for my birthday.*
▶ to request   to demand   to beg for

2 *The police are asking for help to catch the burglar.*
▶ to request   to appeal for

asleep *adjective*

Grandfather was asleep in front of the fire.
▶ sleeping   dozing   resting   slumbering   snoozing
  having a nap

← → An opposite is **awake**.

astonish *verb*

She astonished us with her skilful tricks.
▶ to amaze   to astound

astonished *adjective*
I was astonished when he told me how much his bike cost.
▶ amazed staggered flabbergasted stunned

athlete *noun*
They are very talented athletes.
▶ a sportsman a sportswoman a runner a sprinter
a high jumper a long jumper

athletics *noun*
Do you enjoy doing athletics?
▶ running sprinting hurdles the high jump the long jump
the triple jump

attach *verb*
You must attach the string firmly to the kite.
▶ to fix to fasten to join to connect to tie to stick to glue

attack *verb*
The two robbers attacked them and stole their money.
▶ to assault
to set upon *Two robbers set upon them.*
to ambush (*to jump out from a hiding place and attack someone*)
to mug (*to attack someone and rob them in the street*)

attempt *verb*
He attempted to escape.
▶ to try to make an effort to endeavour

attractive *adjective*
1 *She's a very attractive girl. That's an attractive colour.*
▶ beautiful pretty lovely gorgeous
2 *He's an attractive boy.*
▶ handsome good-looking
◀▶ An opposite is **unattractive**.

a
b
c
d
e
f
g
h
i
j
k
l
m
n
o
p
q
r
s
t
u
v
w
x
y
z

average *adjective*
What is the average number of children in a class?
▶ **normal usual ordinary typical**

avoid *verb*
1 *I'm allergic to cats, so I try to avoid them.*
▶ **to keep away from to steer clear of**
2 *He always tries to avoid doing the washing up.*
▶ **to get out of**

award *noun*
He got a special award for his bravery.
▶ **a prize a reward a trophy a cup a medal**

aware *adjective*
I was aware that someone was watching me.
▶ **conscious**

" " OTHER WAYS OF SAYING *I was aware that someone was watching me.*
I could sense that someone was watching me.
I could feel that someone was watching me.
I knew that someone was watching me.

---

awful *adjective*
What an awful smell!
▶ **terrible dreadful horrible**

awkward *adjective*
1 *The box was big and awkward to carry.*
▶ **difficult**
2 *They arrived at a very awkward time.*
▶ **inconvenient**
3 *He moves in a very awkward way when he dances.*
▶ **clumsy ungainly**

Bb

baby *noun*
> a child   an infant   a toddler

back *noun*
1 *We sat at the back of the room.*
> the rear
2 *Go and stand at the back of the queue.*
> the end   the rear
← → An opposite is **front**.

bad *adjective*
1 *We couldn't play outside because of the bad weather.*
> unpleasant   nasty   terrible   horrible   dreadful
2 *We had some bad news yesterday.*
> terrible   sad   shocking   upsetting
3 *Do you think he's a bad man?*
> wicked   evil   criminal
4 *That was a very bad thing to do.*
> wicked   wrong   sinful
5 *You bad dog!*
> naughty   disobedient
6 *I'm a very bad tennis player.*
> hopeless   useless   poor   terrible
7 *That was a bad mistake.*
> careless   serious   terrible
8 *I hope the food hasn't gone bad.*
> rotten   off   mouldy
9 *There has been a bad accident on the motorway.*
> terrible   awful   dreadful   serious
10 *She's in a very bad mood.*
> grumpy   angry   irritable
11 *I've got a bad knee.*
> sore   injured
12 *I've got a really bad headache.*
> severe   terrible   awful   splitting
← → An opposite is **good**.

badly *adverb*
1 *Our team played badly.*
▶ terribly   appallingly   poorly
2 *Is she badly injured?*
▶ seriously

bad-tempered *adjective*
Don't be so bad-tempered.
▶ grumpy   moody   irritable
←→ An opposite is **good-tempered**.

bag *noun*
She packed her books into her bag.

> **••• SOME TYPES OF BAG**
> | | | |
> |---|---|---|
> | a backpack | a briefcase | a carrier bag |
> | a handbag | a holdall | a rucksack |
> | a satchel | a suitcase | |

baggy *adjective*
He was wearing a pair of baggy trousers.
▶ loose   loose-fitting   large

ball *noun*
1 *She made the dough into the shape of a ball.*
▶ a sphere   a globe
2 *There was a ball to celebrate the marriage of the princess.*
▶ a dance   a party

band *noun*
1 *He plays the drums in a band.*
▶ a group
a brass band (*one with trumpets and other brass instruments*)
an ensemble (*a small group playing musical instruments*)
an orchestra (*a large group playing musical instruments*)
2 *The cave was home to a band of robbers.*
▶ a gang   a group

bang *noun*
We heard a loud bang.
▶ a crash   a thud   a thump   a boom   an explosion

bang *verb*

1 *He banged on the door.*
> ▶ to knock   to rap   to tap   to hammer

2 *I fell and banged my head.*
> ▶ to bump   to knock   to hit   to bash

bar *noun*

There were iron bars on the windows to stop people from escaping.
> ▶ a pole   a rail   a stick   a rod

bare *adjective*

The baby was bare.
> ▶ naked   undressed   nude

barely *adverb*

I was so excited that I could barely speak.
> ▶ hardly   scarcely   only just

barrier *noun*

The police put up a barrier to keep people out.
> ▶ a fence   a railing   a wall   a barricade
> a roadblock (*a barrier across a road*)

base *noun*

1 *There were plants growing along the base of the wall.*
> ▶ the bottom   the foot

2 *The soldiers returned to their base.*
> ▶ a headquarters   a camp

basic *adjective*

You must learn the basic skills first.
> ▶ main   key   essential   elementary

bat *noun*

• • • SOME TYPES OF BAT

a baseball bat   a cricket bat   a golf club
a hockey stick   a tennis racket

a
b
c
d
e
f
g
h
i
j
k
l
m
n
o
p
q
r
s
t
u
v
w
x
y
z

a
b
c
d
e
f
g
h
i
j
k
l
m
n
o
p
q
r
s
t
u
v
w
x
y
z

battle *noun*
There was an important battle here in 1066.
▶ a fight   an attack
   a skirmish (*a small battle*)
   a siege (*when one side is trapped inside a place*)

bay *noun*
The ship took shelter in the bay.
▶ a cove   an inlet

beach *noun*
The children played on the beach.
▶ the sand   the seaside   the seashore   the shore
   the shingle (*a pebbly beach*)

beam *noun*
1 Old oak beams supported the ceiling.
▶ a rafter   a joist   a girder
2 A beam of light shone onto the table.
▶ a ray   a shaft

bear *verb*
1 The ice may not bear your weight.
▶ to support   to hold
2 I can't bear loud music!
▶ to stand   to put up with

beast *noun*
A huge beast roamed the forest.
▶ a creature   a monster   a brute   a wild animal

beat *verb*
1 We beat the other team 6–0.
▶ to defeat
   to thrash (*to beat someone easily*)
   to be victorious over We were victorious over them.
2 It's cruel to beat animals.
▶ to hit   to thrash   to whip
3 Beat the eggs and sugar together.
▶ to mix   to blend   to stir   to whip

beautiful *adjective*

1 *He married the beautiful princess.*
> ▶ **lovely   pretty   fair   attractive**
>   **glamorous** (*beautiful and rich*)
>   **gorgeous** (*very beautiful*)
>   **stunning** (*very beautiful*)
> ←➔ An opposite is **ugly**.

2 *What a beautiful dress!*
> ▶ **lovely   pretty   gorgeous**
> ←➔ An opposite is **ugly**.

3 *The weather was beautiful for sports day.*
> ▶ **lovely   gorgeous   wonderful   fantastic   fine**
> ←➔ An opposite is **awful**.

become *verb*

1 *A tadpole will become a frog.*
> ▶ **to change into   to grow into   to turn into**

2 *He became angry.*
> ▶ **to get   to grow**

bed *noun*

> **•••** SOME TYPES OF BED
>   **a berth** (*a bed on a ship*)
>   **a bunk** (*one of two beds on top of each other*)
>   **a cot** (*a bed with sides for a baby*)
>   **a four-poster bed** (*a bed with curtains around it*)
>   **a hammock** (*a piece of cloth that you hang up and use as a bed*)

beg *verb*

We begged him to let us go.
> ▶ **to plead with** *We pleaded with him to let us go.*
>   **to ask   to implore** *We implored him to let us go.*

begin *verb*

1 *The little girl began to laugh.*
> ▶ **to start**

2 *What time does the film begin?*
> ▶ **to start   to commence**
> ←➔ An opposite is **end**.

beginning noun

I was scared at the beginning of the film.
▶ the start   the opening
←→ An opposite is **ending**.

behave verb

1 *She was behaving rather strangely.*
▶ to act
2 *Make sure you behave at the party.*
▶ to be good   to behave yourself   to be on your best behaviour

behaviour noun

The children's behaviour was excellent.
▶ conduct   manners   attitude

belief noun

People have different religious beliefs.
▶ a faith   an opinion   a view

believe verb

1 *I don't believe you.*
▶ to trust

> **❝❞** OTHER WAYS OF SAYING *I don't believe you.*
> *I think you're wrong.*
> *I think you're lying.*

2 *I believe that she is innocent.*
▶ to think   to be sure   to be convinced
3 *The ancient Greeks believed in many gods.*
▶ to have faith in   to put your faith in

bell noun

Focus on **bell**

SOME WORDS YOU MIGHT USE TO DESCRIBE THE SOUND
THAT A BELL MAKES

to ring	to chime	to tinkle
to jingle	to clang	to jangle
to toll		

belong *verb*

1 *This book belongs to me.*
▸ **to be owned by**

> **"** OTHER WAYS OF SAYING *This book belongs to me.*
> *This book is mine.*
> *This is my book.*
> *I own this book.*
> *This book is my property.*

2 *Ali belongs to the football club.*
▸ **to be a member of to be in** *Ali is in the football club.*
3 *These pencils belong in the cupboard.*
▸ **to go**

belongings *noun*
Be sure to take your belongings when you get off the train.
▸ **possessions property things**

bend *noun*
There are a lot of sharp bends in this road.
▸ **a corner a turn a twist a curve**

bend *verb*

1 *He bent the wire into the correct shape.*
▸ **to twist to curve to curl to coil to wind**
←→ An opposite is **straighten**.
2 *She bent down to tie her shoelaces.*
▸ **to stoop to crouch to duck**

bent *adjective*
The back wheel of the bicycle was bent.
▸ **twisted crooked distorted warped**
←→ An opposite is **straight**.

best *adjective*
She is the best swimmer in the world.
▸ **finest greatest number-one top**
←→ An opposite is **worst**.

better *adjective*
Tom has been ill, but he's better now.
▸ **all right recovered cured**

a
b
c
d
e
f
g
h
i
j
k
l
m
n
o
p
q
r
s
t
u
v
w
x
y
z

a
b
c
d
e
f
g
h
i
j
k
l
m
n
o
p
q
r
s
t
u
v
w
x
y
z

beware *verb*
Beware of the dog.
▶ to be careful of   to watch out for

biased *adjective*
The referee was biased.
▶ unfair   one-sided   prejudiced

bicycle *noun*
▶ a bike   a cycle

> **••••** SOME TYPES OF BICYCLE
> a mountain bike
> a racing bike
> a tandem (*for two people*)
> a tricycle (*with three wheels*)
> a unicycle (*with one wheel*)

big *adjective*

> **!!!!** **big** *is a word that is often overused.*
>
> **1** *London is a big city.*
> ▶ large   huge   enormous   immense
> **2** *They live in a very big house.*
> ▶ large   spacious   roomy   huge   massive
> **3** *He's quite a big boy for his age.*
> ▶ tall   broad   heavy   well-built
> **4** *She gave me a big helping of pudding.*
> ▶ large   generous
> **5** *This shirt is too big for me.*
> ▶ loose   baggy
> **6** *There was a big celebration after the match.*
> ▶ huge   grand   magnificent
> **7** *This is a big day for our school.*
> ▶ important   significant   vital
> ←→ An opposite is **small**.

bird *noun*

🔍 *Focus on* **bird**

SOME FAMILIAR BRITISH BIRDS

blackbird	blue tit	chaffinch
crow	cuckoo	dove
house martin	lark	magpie
pigeon	robin	sparrow
swallow	thrush	woodpecker
wren		

SOME BIRDS OF PREY

buzzard	eagle	hawk
kestrel	kite	owl
vulture		

SOME FARM BIRDS

chicken	duck	goose

SOME WATER BIRDS

flamingo	heron	kingfisher
moorhen	pelican	swan

SOME SEA BIRDS

albatross	puffin	seagull

SOME TROPICAL BIRDS

budgerigar	canary	cockatoo
macaw	magpie	mynah bird
parakeet	parrot	toucan

SOME WORDS YOU MIGHT USE TO DESCRIBE HOW A BIRD
FLIES

to fly	to swoop	to dive
to soar	to glide	to hover
to flit	to dart	

SOME WORDS YOU MIGHT USE TO DESCRIBE HOW A BIRD
SINGS

to sing	to twitter	to chirp
to warble	to screech	to hoot

a
b
c
d
e
f
g
h
i
j
k
l
m
n
o
p
q
r
s
t
u
v
w
x
y
z

biscuit *noun*
> ▶ a cookie
> a cracker (*for eating with cheese*)
> a wafer (*a very thin biscuit*)

bit *noun*

 bit *is a word that is often overused.*

1 *Can I have a bit of chocolate?*
> ▶ a piece   a square   a chunk

2 *Dad cut me a bit of cake.*
> ▶ a piece   a slice
> a sliver (*a thin slice*)
> a wedge (*a thick slice*)

3 *We need one more bit of wood.*
> ▶ a piece   a block   a plank

4 *Write your name on a bit of paper.*
> ▶ a piece   a sheet
> a scrap (*a small piece*)

5 *We had to pick up all the bits of the broken cup.*
> ▶ a piece   a chip   a fragment

6 *Use an old bit of cloth to clean your bike.*
> ▶ a piece   a scrap

7 *There was a bit of water on the floor.*
> ▶ a drop   a puddle

8 *Would you like a bit of ice cream with your pudding?*
> ▶ a lump   a dollop   a scoop

bite *verb*
1 *Be careful that dog doesn't bite you.*
> ▶ to nip   to snap at
2 *Mice have bitten a hole in the carpet.*
> ▶ to chew   to gnaw   to nibble

bitter *adjective*
The medicine had a bitter taste.
> ▶ sour   sharp   acid
← → An opposite is **sweet**.

black *adjective*
1 *It was a cold, black night.*
▶ dark   pitch black   moonless   starless
2 *She had black hair.*
▶ dark   jet black   ebony

blame *verb*
The teacher blamed me for breaking the window.
▶ **to accuse** *The teacher accused me of breaking the window.*
to tell off *The teacher told me off for breaking the window.*
to scold *The teacher scolded me for breaking the window.*

> **❝ ❞ OTHER WAYS OF SAYING** *The teacher blamed me.*
> *The teacher said it was my fault.*
> *The teacher said that I was responsible.*

blank *adjective*
We started with a blank piece of paper.
▶ clean   fresh   unused

blaze *verb*
The fire was blazing merrily.
▶ to burn   to flicker   to glow

blind *adjective*
My grandfather is blind.
▶ visually impaired

blob *noun*
There was a blob of jam on the table.
▶ a lump   a dollop   a drop

block *noun*
They covered the hole with a block of concrete.
▶ a piece   a lump   a slab

block *verb*
A huge lorry had blocked the road.
▶ to obstruct   to clog up

blow *verb*
He blew on his food to cool it down.
▶ to breathe   to puff

blow up verb
1 *Shall I help you blow up the balloons?*
▶ to inflate
2 *The car blew up.*
▶ to explode

blue adjective
▶ **navy blue sky-blue royal blue turquoise
azure** (*bright blue*)

blush verb
She blushed whenever a boy spoke to her.
▶ **to go red to redden to flush**

boast verb
He's always boasting about how good he is at football.
▶ **to brag to show off to gloat**

boat noun
▶ **a ship** (*a large boat*) **a vessel** (*a large boat*)
a craft (*a small boat*)

🔍 *Focus on* **boat**

SOME TYPES OF BOAT

an aircraft carrier	**a barge**	**a battleship**
a canoe	**a dinghy**	**a ferry**
a fishing boat	**a lifeboat**	**a motor boat**
a raft	**a rowing boat**	**a sailing boat**
a speed boat	**a submarine**	**a tanker**
a trawler	**a warship**	**a yacht**

SOME WORDS YOU MIGHT USE TO DESCRIBE HOW A BOAT MOVES

to sail	**to float**	**to glide**
to bob up and down	**to drift**	**to speed along**
to chug along		

---

bog noun
They didn't want to get lost in the bog.
▶ **a marsh a swamp**

boggy adjective
The ground was very boggy.
▶ **wet soft sticky marshy**

boil *verb*
Is the water boiling yet?
▶ to bubble   to simmer

boiling *adjective*
1 *It was a boiling hot day.*
▶ hot   baking   scorching   sweltering
2 *The radiator's boiling!*
▶ hot   red hot

bolt *verb*
1 *He bolted the door.*
▶ to lock   to fasten
2 *The horse bolted.*
▶ to run away   to flee
3 *She bolted her food.*
▶ to gobble down   to guzzle   to wolf

book *noun*
He was reading a book.
▶ a novel   a story book   a poetry book   a picture book
a non-fiction book   a textbook

••• SOME TYPES OF READING MATERIAL		
an atlas	a brochure	a catalogue
a dictionary	a directory	an encyclopedia
a magazine	a thesaurus	

bored *adjective*
I'm bored with this!
▶ fed up   tired *I'm tired of this.*

boring *adjective*
1 *This programme is really boring!*
▶ dull   tedious
2 *It was a really boring day.*
▶ tedious   humdrum   uneventful   unexciting
◀ ▶ An opposite is **interesting**.

a b c d e f g h i j k l m n o p q r s t u v w x y z

borrow *verb*
Can I borrow your pen for a minute, please?
▶ to use   to take

> **6 9** ANOTHER WAY OF SAYING *Can I borrow your pen?*
> *Will you lend me your pen?*

boss *noun*
1 *Who's the boss here?*
▶ the person in charge   the leader   the chief   the head
2 *Her boss said she could have the day off.*
▶ an employer   a manager   a supervisor   a director

bossy *adjective*
She can be bossy sometimes.
▶ domineering   bullying

bother *verb*
1 *Is the loud music bothering you?*
▶ to annoy   to disturb   to upset   to irritate
2 *They didn't bother to clear up their mess.*
▶ to make the effort   to take the trouble

bottom *noun*
1 *We'll wait at the bottom of the hill.*
▶ the foot   the base
← → An opposite is **top**.
2 *She fell and landed on her bottom.*
▶ backside   rear

bounce *verb*
The ball bounced off the wall.
▶ to rebound   to ricochet

bound *adjective*
We're bound to win.
▶ certain   sure

a
b
c
d
e
f
g
h
i
j
k
l
m
n
o
p
q
r
s
t
u
v
w
x
y
z

bowl *noun*
She put the fruit into a bowl.
▶ a dish   a basin

box *noun*
1 I bought a box of cereal.
▶ a packet   a carton
2 We packed the books into a box.
▶ a case   a crate   a chest   a trunk

boy *noun*
▶ a lad   a kid   a child   a youngster
a youth (*a teenage boy*)   a teenager

brain *noun*
He's got a very good brain.
▶ a mind

branch *noun*
A large branch had fallen off the tree.
▶ a bough

brand *noun*
He likes expensive brands of trainers.
▶ a make   a sort   a label

brave *adjective*
1 A brave knight came to the rescue.
▶ courageous   bold   heroic   valiant   gallant   intrepid
plucky   fearless
2 He wasn't brave enough to go over the bridge.
▶ courageous   daring   adventurous
← → An opposite is **cowardly**.

bravery *noun*
He got a medal for his bravery.
▶ courage   heroism   valour
← → An opposite is **cowardice**.

a b c d e f g h i j k l m n o p q r s t u v w x y z

a

b

c

d

e

f

g

h

i

j

k

l

m

n

o

p

q

r

s

t

u

v

w

x

y

z

break *verb*

1 *I dropped a cup and it broke.*
  ▶ **to smash   to crack   to shatter**

2 *The stick broke in two.*
  ▶ **to snap   to split**

3 *The bridge broke.*
  ▶ **to collapse**

4 *My brother broke my CD player.*
  ▶ **to damage   to wreck   to ruin**

5 *She fell and broke her wrist.*
  ▶ **to fracture**

6 *You will be punished if you break the rules.*
  ▶ **to disobey**

7 *Someone had deliberately broken the seat.*
  ▶ **to damage   to vandalize   to sabotage**

break *noun*

1 *We climbed through a break in the hedge.*
  ▶ **a gap   a hole   an opening**

2 *There was a break in the pipe.*
  ▶ **a crack   a split   a hole**

3 *We'll stop for a short break.*
  ▶ **a rest   a pause**

4 *There will be a fifteen-minute break halfway through the show.*
  ▶ **an interval   an intermission**

break off *verb*

1 *The strap on my bag has broken off.*
  ▶ **to fall off   to come off   to drop off   to snap off**

2 *She picked up the bar of chocolate and broke a piece off.*
  ▶ **to pull off   to cut off   to snap off   to rip off   to tear off**

bridge *noun*

• • •   SOME TYPES OF BRIDGE

    a flyover (*over a motorway*)
    a footbridge (*for people*)
    a viaduct (*over a river or valley*)

---

brief *adjective*

1 *We only had time for a brief visit.*
  ▶ **short quick fleeting** (*very brief*)
2 *He wrote a brief letter to his aunt.*
  ▶ **short concise**
←→ An opposite is **long**.

bright *adjective*

1 *We saw a bright light in the sky.*
  ▶ **shining dazzling gleaming sparkling glittering**
  blinding (*very bright*)
  brilliant (*very bright*)
←→ An opposite is **dull**.

2 *I like wearing bright colours.*
  ▶ **vivid strong rich**
←→ An opposite is **dull**.

3 *It was a lovely bright day.*
  ▶ **clear fine sunny**
←→ An opposite is **gloomy**.

4 *He's a very bright boy.*
  ▶ **clever intelligent brainy quick sharp smart**
←→ An opposite is **stupid**.

brilliant *adjective*

1 *He is a brilliant scientist.*
  ▶ **intelligent clever talented**
←→ An opposite is **stupid**.

2 *It's a brilliant film.*
  ▶ **great excellent wonderful fantastic marvellous**
←→ An opposite is **terrible**.

bring *verb*

1 *I'll bring the shopping in.*
  ▶ **to carry to take**
2 *Please bring me a drink.*
  ▶ **to get to fetch**

broad *adjective*

The river is quite broad here.
  ▶ **wide big large**
←→ An opposite is **narrow**.

brown

brown *adjective*
He was wearing brown trousers.
▶ beige fawn khaki chocolate brown

brush *verb*
We had to brush the floor.
▶ to sweep to clean

bubbles *noun*
She picked up a handful of bubbles from the bath.
▶ foam lather suds

bucket *noun*
▶ a pail

bug *noun*
1 *You can find lots of interesting bugs in your garden.*
▶ an insect a creepy-crawly *(informal)*
2 *She has been off school with a bug.*
▶ a virus a germ an illness
3 *The computer program had a bug in it.*
▶ a fault an error a virus

build *verb*
1 *It takes about six months to build a new house.*
▶ to construct to put up
2 *He loves building model aeroplanes.*
▶ to make to construct

bully *verb*
Some of the older boys were bullying him.
▶ to tease to frighten to threaten to persecute

bump *noun*
1 *The book fell to the ground with a bump.*
▶ a bang a crash a thud a thump
2 *She's got a nasty bump on her head.*
▶ a lump a swelling

bump *verb*
I fell and bumped my head.
▶ to bang to knock to hit to bash

bumpy *adjective*
We drove along the bumpy road.
▶ rough   uneven

bunch *noun*
1 He bought me a bunch of flowers.
▶ a bouquet   a posy
2 She handed me a large bunch of keys.
▶ a collection   a set   a quantity
3 I went to the cinema with a bunch of friends.
▶ a group   a crowd   a gang

bundle *noun*
He brought a bundle of old newspapers.
▶ a pile   a heap

burglar *noun*
The police arrested the burglars.
▶ a robber   a thief   an intruder   a housebreaker

burn *verb*
1 Paper burns easily.
▶ to catch fire   to catch light   to burst into flames
2 The fire was burning in the grate.
▶ to blaze   to glow
to smoulder (*to burn slowly*)
to flicker (*to burn with small flames*)
3 We can burn all this rubbish.
▶ to set fire to   to set alight   to incinerate
to cremate (*to burn the body of a dead person*)
4 He burnt his shirt on the iron.
▶ to scorch   to singe

burst *verb*
My balloon's burst!
▶ to pop   to go bang   to split

bus *noun*
▶ a coach   a minibus

bush *noun*
We hid in the bushes.
▶ a shrub

a
b
c
d
e
f
g
h
i
j
k
l
m
n
o
p
q
r
s
t
u
v
w
x
y
z

business *noun*

1 *Her dad works in business.*
▶ commerce industry trade
2 *His parents run their own business.*
▶ a company a firm an organization

busy *adjective*

1 *I've been very busy this morning.*
▶ active energetic
←→ An opposite is **idle**.
2 *Dad was busy in the garden.*
▶ occupied working active
←→ An opposite is **idle**.
3 *London is a very busy place.*
▶ crowded bustling lively
←→ An opposite is **peaceful**.

buy *verb*

1 *Where's the best place to buy a bike?*
▶ to get to obtain to purchase
2 *My friend bought me some sweets.*
▶ to get *My friend got me some sweets.*
to treat someone to *My friend treated me to some sweets.*
to pay for *My friend paid for some sweets for me.*
←→ An opposite is **sell**.

Cc

cabin *noun*
They lived in a log cabin.
▶ a hut   a chalet   a shed

cable *noun*
The electric cables had been cut.
▶ a wire   a lead

cafe *noun*
We stopped at a cafe for lunch.
▶ a restaurant   a snack bar   a cafeteria
a canteen (*in a school or office*)

cage *noun*
I think it's cruel to keep animals in cages.
▶ a hutch (*for rabbits*)
an enclosure (*in a zoo*)
an aviary (*for birds*)
a pen (*for farm animals*)

calculate *verb*
Can you calculate the amount we have to pay?
▶ to work out   to add up

call *verb*
1 *'Hello,' she called.*
▶ to shout   to yell   to cry
2 *Mum called us in when it started to rain.*
▶ to send for *Mum sent for us when it started to rain.*
3 *We've decided to call the puppy Lucky.*
▶ to name
4 *I'll call you when I get home.*
▶ to phone   to ring   to telephone
to give someone a ring *I'll give you a ring when I get home.*

a
b
c
d
e
f
g
h
i
j
k
l
m
n
o
p
q
r
s
t
u
v
w
x
y
z

calm *adjective*

  1 *The sea was very calm.*
    ▶ still flat smooth still
    ←→ An opposite is **stormy**.
  2 *It was a lovely calm day.*
    ▶ still windless
    ←→ An opposite is **windy**.
  3 *She told the children to keep calm.*
    ▶ quiet relaxed cool patient
    ←→ An opposite is **excited**.

camera *noun*

> **•••** SOME TYPES OF CAMERA
>   a camcorder   a digital camera
>   a video camera

cancel *verb*
We had to cancel the football match.
    ▶ to call off to abandon
    to postpone (*to cancel it until a later time*)

capture *verb*
The police have captured the robbers.
    ▶ to catch to arrest
    to take prisoner *The police have taken the robbers prisoner.*

car *noun*

> 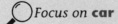 *Focus on **car***
>
>   ▶ a motor car an automobile
>
> SOME TYPES OF CAR
>   an estate car   a four-wheel drive (4x4)
>   a hatchback   a people carrier   a racing car
>   a saloon   a sports car   a van
>
> SOME WORDS YOU MIGHT USE TO DESCRIBE HOW A CAR MOVES
>   to accelerate   to speed up   to slow down
>   to speed along   to race   to zoom
>   to whizz   to crawl along

care noun

1 *Take care. It's a very busy road.*

> **OTHER WAYS OF SAYING** *Take care.*
> *Be careful.*
> *Pay attention.*
> *Look out.*

2 *Take care of your little brother.*

> **OTHER WAYS OF SAYING** *Take care of him.*
> *Look after him.*
> *Protect him.*
> *Care for him.*

care verb

1 *I don't care who wins the game.*
> ▸ **to mind** *I don't mind who wins.*
> **to be bothered** *I'm not bothered who wins.*

2 *We should care about our planet.*
> ▸ **to be concerned about**

careful adjective

1 *Be careful when you cross the busy road.*
> ▸ **cautious   alert   attentive**

> **OTHER WAYS OF SAYING** *Be careful.*
> *Take care.*
> *Look out.*
> *Pay attention.*
> *Mind.*

2 *This is good, careful work.*
> ▸ **neat   thorough   conscientious   painstaking**
> **accurate**

← → An opposite is **careless**.

a b c d e f g h i j k l m n o p q r s t u v w x y z

careless *adjective*

1 *This work is untidy and careless!*
▶ **messy   untidy   sloppy   shoddy**

2 *You have made some careless mistakes.*
▶ **silly   sloppy**

3 *She was careless and left the door open.*
▶ **foolish   thoughtless   irresponsible**
◀▶ An opposite is **careful**.

carnival *noun*
▶ **a festival   a celebration   a parade   a procession**

carry *verb*
We carried the boxes into the house.
▶ **to lift   to move   to bring   to take**

carry on *verb*
The children carried on talking.
▶ **to continue   to keep on   to go on**

cart *noun*
1 *We loaded the vegetables onto a cart.*
▶ **a wagon   a trailer**
2 *He pushed the small cart through the streets.*
▶ **a barrow   a wheelbarrow**

case *noun*
1 *We packed the books into wooden cases.*
▶ **a box   a crate   a container**
2 *He left his case on the train.*
▶ **a suitcase   a bag   a holdall   a trunk   a rucksack**

castle *noun*
▶ **a fort   a fortress   a stronghold**

cat *noun*

⚲ *Focus on* **cat**

> ▶ a pussy a pussy cat a moggy a kitten (*a young cat*)
> a tomcat (*a male cat*)

SOME TYPES OF DOMESTIC CAT
a Manx cat a Persian cat
a Siamese cat a tabby cat
a tortoiseshell cat

SOME TYPES OF WILD CAT
a cheetah a leopard a lion
a lynx an ocelot a panther
a puma a tiger

SOME WORDS YOU MIGHT USE TO DESCRIBE HOW A CAT
WALKS, RUNS, OR JUMPS
to creep to pad to prowl
to slink to crouch to pounce
to spring

SOME WORDS YOU MIGHT USE TO DESCRIBE THE SOUNDS
A CAT MAKES
to miaow to mew to purr
to hiss to spit

---

catch *verb*

1 *The police have caught the thieves.*
> ▶ to capture to arrest
> to take prisoner *The police have taken the thieves prisoner.*

2 *We caught wild rabbits to eat.*
> ▶ to trap to snare

3 *I've caught a fish!*
> ▶ to hook to net

4 *Try to catch the ball.*
> ▶ to get hold of to take hold of to hold to grip to grab

5 *She caught chickenpox.*
> ▶ to get to be infected with to contract

6 *We caught the bus into town.*
> ▶ to get to travel on

a
b
c
d
e
f
g
h
i
j
k
l
m
n
o
p
q
r
s
t
u
v
w
x
y
z

catching *adjective*
I hope your cold isn't catching.
▶ infectious   contagious

cause *verb*
The heavy rain caused a lot of flooding.
▶ to bring about   to lead to   to result in   to produce

cave *noun*
▶ a cavern   a grotto

celebration *noun*
There was a huge celebration when the new king was crowned.
▶ a party   a feast   a carnival

centre *noun*
1 *There was a fire in the centre of the room.*
▶ the middle
2 *They live right in the centre of the city.*
▶ the middle   the heart
3 *The centre of the planet is very hot.*
▶ the core   the middle

certain *adjective*
1 *I'm certain I saw her in town.*
▶ sure   positive   convinced
← → An opposite is **uncertain**.
2 *A certain person is going to be very cross about this.*
▶ particular

chair *noun*
He sat in his usual chair by the fire.
▶ a seat

● ● ● SOME TYPES OF CHAIR		
an armchair	a bench	a couch
a deckchair	a rocking chair	a settee
a sofa	a stool	

champion *noun*
I want to win the competition and become the champion.
▶ the winner   the best   the victor

chance *noun*
1 *This is our last chance to escape.*
▶ an opportunity
2 *There is a chance that we will fail.*
▶ a possibility   a risk
3 *We met by chance.*
▶ luck   coincidence   fate

change *noun*
1 *Have you got some change for the sweet machine?*
▶ coins   loose change
2 *At the weekend there will be a change in the weather.*
▶ an alteration

change *verb*
1 *Our school has changed a lot in the last ten years.*
▶ to alter
2 *Tadpoles change into frogs.*
▶ to turn into   to become
3 *The witch changed him into a mouse.*
▶ to turn   to transform
4 *My design didn't work, so I had to change it.*
▶ to alter   to modify   to adjust
5 *I took the dress back to the shop and changed it.*
▶ to exchange   to swap

chaos *noun*
There was chaos when the lights went out.
▶ confusion   pandemonium   mayhem

character *noun*
1 *Which character in the pantomime do you want to play?*
▶ a part   a role
2 *Tom has got a lovely character.*
▶ a personality   a nature   a temperament

a
b
c
d
e
f
g
h
i
j
k
l
m
n
o
p
q
r
s
t
u
v
w
x
y
z

a
b
c
d
e
f
g
h
i
j
k
l
m
n
o
p
q
r
s
t
u
v
w
x
y
z

charge noun

1 *There is no charge to go into the museum.*
▶ **a fee   a payment**

2 *I am in charge of the ice cream stall.*

> **" "** OTHER WAYS OF SAYING *I am in charge of it.*
> *I run it.*
> *I organize it.*
> *I deal with it.*
> *I manage it.*

charge verb

1 *How much do they charge for orange juice?*
▶ **to ask**

2 *The bull was about to charge.*
▶ **to attack   to rush   to stampede**

charming adjective

What a charming little dog!
▶ **lovely   pretty   beautiful   delightful   cute**

chart noun

1 *We made a chart to show how tall the children in our class are.*
▶ **a graph   a diagram   a table**

2 *Ancient sailors used charts of the stars to find their way.*
▶ **a map**

chase verb

1 *The dog chased us down the road.*
▶ **to run after   to follow   to pursue**

2 *It is natural for cats to chase birds.*
▶ **to hunt   to track   to catch**

chat verb

Stop chatting!
▶ **to chatter   to talk   to natter**
to gossip (*to chat about other people*)

cheap *adjective*
These trainers are quite cheap.
▶ inexpensive   reasonable   not very expensive
cut-price
← → An opposite is **expensive**.

cheat *verb*
1 *The other team won, but they cheated!*
▶ to break the rules   to not play fair
2 *They cheated me out of my money.*
▶ to trick   to swindle   to fool

check *verb*
Always check your spellings.
▶ to look at   to examine
to double-check (*to check twice*)

cheeky *adjective*
Don't be so cheeky!
▶ rude   impertinent   impudent   insolent
disrespectful
← → An opposite is **respectful**.

cheer *verb*
Everyone cheered when our team scored.
▶ to shout   to shout hurray   to applaud

cheerful *adjective*
He seems very cheerful today.
▶ happy   smiling   joyful   light-hearted   in a good mood
← → An opposite is **sad**.

chew *verb*
1 *She was chewing on a sweet.*
▶ to bite   to crunch   to suck   to munch   to nibble
2 *Mice had chewed through the wires.*
▶ to bite   to gnaw   to nibble

chief *noun*
Who is the chief around here?
▶ the boss   the leader

chief *adjective*
Safety is our chief concern.
▶ main   most important   key   principal

child *noun*
▶ a boy   a girl   a kid   a youngster
a brat (*an irritating child*)
a toddler (*a very young child*)

childish *adjective*
This behaviour is very childish!
▶ silly   immature   juvenile   babyish
←→ An opposite is **mature**.

chilly *adjective*
1 The water is quite chilly.
▶ cold   cool
2 The weather's a bit chilly.
▶ cold   nippy   cool   fresh   frosty   wintry
←→ An opposite is **warm**.

choice *noun*
1 You can have first choice.
▶ pick
2 There's a choice of vanilla, strawberry, and chocolate ice cream.
▶ a selection

choke *verb*
1 The thick smoke was choking us.
▶ to suffocate   to asphyxiate
2 The tight collar was choking him.
▶ to strangle   to throttle

choose verb
Which cake shall I choose?
▶ to pick   to select   to decide on

chop verb
My dad was chopping wood.
▶ to cut   to saw   to split

chubby adjective
You were quite a chubby baby.
▶ plump   podgy   tubby

chunk noun
He gave me a slice of bread and a chunk of cheese.
▶ a piece   a lump   a block   a wedge

cinema noun
We're going to the cinema this evening.
▶ the pictures   the movies

circle noun
We all sat round in a circle.
▶ a ring

citizen noun
All the citizens of the town came to the meeting.
▶ a person   a resident   an inhabitant

claim verb
She walked up to claim her prize.
▶ to ask for   to request   to demand

clap verb
The audience clapped.
▶ to applaud   to cheer

class noun
Which class are you in?
▶ a form   a group   a set

clean

clean *adjective*

1 *Her hair was always tidy and her clothes were clean.*
> ▶ spotless
> ←→ An opposite is **dirty**.

2 *Make sure your bedroom is nice and clean.*
> ▶ tidy   spick and span
> ←→ An opposite is **untidy**.

3 *The water in this river is very clean.*
> ▶ fresh   pure   clear   unpolluted
> ←→ An opposite is **polluted**.

4 *Start again on a clean sheet of paper.*
> ▶ blank   unused   fresh   new

clean *verb*

1 *They had to stay at home and clean the floors.*
> ▶ to brush   to sweep   to wipe   to hoover   to wash   to mop
> to scrub

2 *Someone comes in and cleans the tables every morning.*
> ▶ to dust   to wipe   to polish

3 *Go and clean your hands.*
> ▶ to wash   to scrub   to rinse

4 *Don't forget to clean your teeth.*
> ▶ to brush

clear *adjective*

1 *Windows are usually made of clear glass.*
> ▶ see-through   transparent
> ←→ An opposite is **opaque**.

2 *The water in the lake was lovely and clear.*
> ▶ clean   pure
> ←→ An opposite is **dirty**.

3 *The next morning the sky was clear.*
> ▶ blue   sunny   cloudless
> ←→ An opposite is **cloudy**.

4 *The teacher said something, but it wasn't very clear.*
> ▶ audible   distinct   understandable

5 *We can get this channel on our TV, but the picture isn't very clear.*
> ▶ good   easy to see

▶▶

6 *A tree fell across the road yesterday, but the road is clear now.*
▶ **unblocked**
←→ An opposite is **blocked**.

7 *I want you to tidy up all this mess. Is that clear?*
▶ **plain understandable**

clear *verb*

We need to clear these chairs out of the way.
▶ **to move to take away**

clever *adjective*

1 *You're so clever!*
▶ **intelligent bright brainy quick sharp smart**
2 *The old man was very clever and knew what to do.*
▶ **wise sensible**
3 *That's a very clever idea.*
▶ **good brilliant**
4 *He showed us some clever magic tricks.*
▶ **good great cunning crafty ingenious**
←→ An opposite is **stupid**.

climb *verb*

1 *He climbed the stairs.*
▶ **to go up to run up**
2 *The plane climbed into the air.*
▶ **to rise to ascend to go up**
3 *They climbed over the rocks.*
▶ **to clamber to scramble**

cling *verb*

He was clinging to the handrail.
▶ **to hold onto to grip to grasp**

clip *verb*

I think we need to clip the hedge.
▶ **to cut to trim**

clock *noun*

... SOME TYPES OF CLOCK

an alarm clock	a cuckoo clock
a digital clock	a grandfather clock
a travelling clock (*one that folds into a case*)	

close

a
b
c
d
e
f
g
h
i
j
k
l
m
n
o
p
q
r
s
t
u
v
w
x
y
z

close *adjective*

1 *He sat close to the fire.*
> ▶ **near to   next to   beside**
> ←→ An opposite is **far away**.

2 *I took a close look at the map.*
> ▶ **careful   detailed**

close *verb*

Please close the door.
> ▶ **to shut   to lock   to slam** (*to close noisily*)
> ←→ An opposite is **open**.

clothes *noun*

He was dressed in old-fashioned clothes.
> ▶ **attire** *He was dressed in old-fashioned attire.*

∙∙∙ SOME CLOTHES FOR WARM WEATHER

a blouse	a dress	a shirt
shorts	a skirt	a sunhat
trousers	a t-shirt	

SOME CLOTHES FOR COLD WEATHER

an anorak	a cardigan	a cloak
a coat	a duffel coat	a fleece
gloves	a jumper	mittens
a muffler	a pullover	a raincoat
a scarf	a sweater	a sweatshirt
a woolly hat		

SOME SMART CLOTHES

a blazer	a jacket	a suit
a tie	a uniform	a waistcoat

SOME INFORMAL CLOTHES

dungarees	jeans	a jogging suit
leggings	a sweatshirt	a t-shirt
a tracksuit		

SOME CLOTHES FROM AROUND THE WORLD

a kimono	a salwar kameez	a sari
a sarong	a djelleba	a yashmak

---

cloudy *adjective*
It was a cloudy day.
▶ grey dull overcast gloomy
←→ An opposite is **clear**.

club *noun*
She joined her local drama club.
▶ a society a group an association

clue *noun*
The police have found one important clue.
▶ an indication a sign a piece of evidence

clumsy *adjective*
I can be quite clumsy sometimes.
▶ careless accident-prone

coach *noun*
1 *We went to London on the coach.*
▶ a bus
2 *A football coach trains the team.*
▶ a trainer an instructor

coil *verb*
She coiled the rope around a tree.
▶ to wind to loop to twist to curl

cold *adjective*
1 *It's quite cold outside today.*
▶ chilly cool nippy frosty icy snowy wintry
freezing *(very cold)*
bitter *(very cold)*
2 *I'm cold!*
▶ chilly
freezing *(very cold)*
frozen *(very cold)*
3 *The water in the pool was very cold.*
▶ chilly freezing *(very cold)*
4 *This soup is cold!*
▶ stone cold
←→ An opposite is **hot**.

a
b
c
d
e
f
g
h
i
j
k
l
m
n
o
p
q
r
s
t
u
v
w
x
y
z

collapse *verb*

1 *Some of the old buildings collapsed in the storm.*
▶ to fall down   to cave in

2 *The old man collapsed in the street.*
▶ to faint   to pass out   to fall down

collect *verb*

1 *I collect old coins.*
▶ to keep   to save

2 *We have collected a lot of things for our nature table.*
▶ to accumulate   to bring together

3 *Collect all your things together and then we can leave.*
▶ to gather together   to get together
  to pick up

4 *My mum collected me from school.*
▶ to fetch   to pick up

collection *noun*

He's got a huge collection of CDs.
▶ a set   a hoard   an assortment

college *noun*

I'm going to go to college when I leave school.
▶ university

collide *verb*

Their car collided with a van.
▶ to hit   to bump into   to crash into
  to smash into

colour *noun*

I think we should paint the room a different colour.
▶ a shade

▶▶

colour noun (continued)

> SOME SHADES OF RED
> crimson   maroon   ruby
> scarlet
>
> SOME SHADES OF BLUE
> aquamarine   azure   navy blue
> royal blue   sapphire   sky blue
> turquoise
>
> SOME SHADES OF GREEN
> emerald   lime green   bottle green
> racing green
>
> SOME SHADES OF YELLOW
> lemon   gold   primrose
>
> SOME SHADES OF BLACK
> ebony   jet black
>
> SOME SHADES OF WHITE
> cream   ivory   snow white
>
> SOME SHADES OF GREY
> charcoal grey   dove grey   silver
>
> SOME SHADES OF BROWN
> beige   bronze   chocolate
> fawn   khaki   tan

colourful adjective

Everyone was wearing colourful clothes.
> ▶ bright multicoloured cheerful
> ← → An opposite is **dull**.

combine verb

1 *Combine all the ingredients in a bowl.*
> ▶ to put together to mix together to add together to blend

2 *The two groups combined to make one big group.*
> ▶ to come together to join together to unite to merge

a
b
c
d
e
f
g
h
i
j
k
l
m
n
o
p
q
r
s
t
u
v
w
x
y
z

come *verb*

1 *We saw a car coming towards us.*
▶ **to move   to approach** *We saw a car approaching us.*
to draw near *We saw a car drawing near to us.*

2 *Would you like to come to my house?*
▶ **to visit**

3 *A letter came this morning.*
▶ **to arrive   to turn up**

comfort *verb*

I comforted the little boy because he was upset.
▶ **to reassure   to calm down   to cheer up**

comfortable *adjective*

1 *This chair is very comfortable.*
▶ **soft   cosy   relaxing**

2 *Are you comfortable there?*
▶ **relaxed   cosy   warm   happy   snug**
◀▶ An opposite is **uncomfortable**.

command *verb*

She commanded us to leave.
▶ **to tell   to order   to instruct**

comment *noun*

One of the boys kept making silly comments.
▶ **a remark   an observation**

commit *verb*

He has committed a terrible crime.
▶ **to carry out**
to be guilty of *He is guilty of a terrible crime.*

common *adjective*

1 *These birds are quite common in Europe.*
▶ **widespread**

> **" "   OTHER WAYS OF SAYING** *These birds are quite common.*
> *You see a lot of these birds.*
> *These birds are quite commonly found.*   ▶▶

2 *Earthquakes are common in this part of the world.*
▶ **frequent**

> **❝❞ OTHER WAYS OF SAYING** *Earthquakes are common.*
> *Earthquakes happen quite often.*
> *There are a lot of earthquakes.*

3 *Having your tonsils out is a common operation.*
▶ **routine   standard**
4 *It is very common for children to feel nervous before injections.*
▶ **ordinary   usual   normal**
←→ An opposite is **rare**.

commotion *noun*
There was a terrible commotion.
▶ **an uproar   a row   confusion   chaos**

company *noun*
1 *I took my sister with me for company.*
▶ **friendship   companionship**
2 *They run a company that makes sweets and biscuits.*
▶ **a business   a factory   a firm**

compare *verb*
Please compare the two stories.
▶ **to contrast**

competition *noun*
1 *We've entered a poetry competition.*
▶ **a contest**
2 *Our team won the football competition.*
▶ **a tournament   a championship**

complain *verb*
Everyone complained about the food.
▶ **to moan   to grumble   to whinge**

a
b
c
d
e
f
g
h
i
j
k
l
m
n
o
p
q
r
s
t
u
v
w
x
y
z

a
b
c
d
e
f
g
h
i
j
k
l
m
n
o
p
q
r
s
t
u
v
w
x
y
z

complete adjective

1 *I haven't got a complete set.*
▶ **full   whole**
←→ An opposite is **incomplete**.

2 *At last the work was complete.*
▶ **finished**
←→ An opposite is **unfinished**.

3 *The show was a complete disaster.*
▶ **total   absolute   utter**

completely adverb

I'm completely exhausted!
▶ **totally   utterly   absolutely**

complicated adjective

1 *This is a very complicated machine.*
▶ **complex   sophisticated   intricate**

2 *We had to do some complicated sums.*
▶ **difficult   hard**
←→ An opposite is **simple**.

computer noun

••• SOME TYPES OF COMPUTER	
a desktop	a laptop
a notebook	a PC
a palm top	a personal computer
a portable computer	

concentrate verb

1 *There was so much noise that I couldn't concentrate.*
▶ **to think   to work**

2 *Sit down and concentrate on your work.*
▶ **to pay attention to   to think about   to focus on**

concern *verb*
This doesn't concern you.
▶ to affect   to involve

> OTHER WAYS OF SAYING *This doesn't concern you.*
> *This is nothing to do with you.*
> *This doesn't matter to you.*
> *This is none of your business.*

concerned *adjective*
We were all very concerned about you.
▶ worried   anxious

condemn *verb*
The judge condemned him to death.
▶ to sentence

condition *noun*
The amount your bike is worth will depend on the condition it is in.
▶ the state

> OTHER WAYS OF SAYING *It is in good condition.*
> *It is quite new.*
> *It is in good working order.*
>
> OTHER WAYS OF SAYING *It is in bad condition.*
> *It is old.*
> *It is broken.*
> *It is tatty.*
> *It doesn't work properly.*

confess *verb*
She confessed that she had stolen the money.
▶ to admit   to own up   to tell the truth

confident *adjective*
1 She looked very calm and confident.
▶ self-assured   unafraid
2 We are confident that we can win.
▶ sure   certain

a b c d e f g h i j k l m n o p q r s t u v w x y z

confuse

confuse verb
The instructions for the game confused me.
▶ to puzzle to baffle to bewilder to perplex

confused adjective
I was feeling very confused.
▶ puzzled bewildered baffled

congratulate verb
I congratulated Salim on winning the race.
▶ to compliment

connect verb
You need to connect this wire to the battery.
▶ to join to attach to fix

considerate adjective
Please try to be more considerate.
▶ thoughtful kind helpful unselfish
← → An opposite is **selfish**.

constant adjective
I'm fed up with this constant noise.
▶ incessant continuous relentless never-ending

construct verb
We constructed a model aeroplane.
▶ to build to make to assemble

contain verb
The bag contained some gold coins.
▶ to hold to have inside

contest noun
We're having a jumping contest.
▶ a competition a match a championship

continual adjective
Stop this continual arguing!
▶ constant repeated incessant

continue *verb*

1 *Continue reading until the end of the chapter.*
▸ to go on   to carry on   to keep on
2 *The rain continued all afternoon.*
▸ to go on   to carry on   to last

continuous *adjective*
In the factory there was the continuous noise of machines.
▸ constant   incessant

contribute *verb*

1 *They contributed money to the school repair fund.*
▸ to give   to donate
to make a donation *They made a donation to the school repair fund.*
2 *He contributed ideas to the class discussion.*
▸ to add   to put forward

control *verb*
The pilot uses these levers to control the aeroplane.
▸ to guide   to move   to direct

convenient *adjective*
The shop is just around the corner, so it's quite convenient.
▸ handy   useful
◂▸ An opposite is **inconvenient**.

conversation *noun*
We had a long conversation about sport.
▸ a talk   a discussion   a chat

convince *verb*
My dad finally convinced me that ghosts are not real.
▸ to persuade

convinced *adjective*
I'm convinced that she is lying.
▸ sure   certain

a
b
c
d
e
f
g
h
i
j
k
l
m
n
o
p
q
r
s
t
u
v
w
x
y
z

cook *verb*

> 🔍 Focus on **cook**
>
> **SOME WAYS TO COOK MEAT**
> to roast   to fry   to grill
> to barbecue   to stew   to casserole
>
> **SOME WAYS TO COOK BREAD OR CAKES**
> to bake   to toast
>
> **SOME WAYS TO COOK VEGETABLES**
> to boil   to steam   to simmer
> to stir-fry   to bake   to roast
>
> **SOME WAYS TO COOK EGGS**
> to boil   to poach   to scramble
> to fry

cool *adjective*
1 *It's quite cool outside today.*
  ▶ cold   chilly   nippy
2 *I could do with a nice cool drink.*
  ▶ cold   ice-cold
← → An opposite is **hot**.

cope *verb*
Can you cope with all this work?
  ▶ to **manage** *Can you manage all this work?*

copy *verb*
1 *See if you can copy this picture.*
  ▶ to reproduce   to make a copy of
2 *The teacher waved, and we all copied her.*
  ▶ to imitate   to do the same as *We all did the same as her.*

corner *noun*
1 *I'll meet you on the corner, by the school.*
  ▶ a crossroads   a turning   a junction
2 *Don't drive too fast, there's a corner up ahead*
  ▶ a bend

correct *adjective*
1 *That is the correct answer.*
  ▶ **right**
2 *Make sure all your spellings are correct.*
  ▶ **right   accurate   exact**
← → An opposite is **wrong**.

correct *verb*
Shall I correct my mistakes?
  ▶ **to put right   to rectify**

cost *verb*

> ❝ ❞ OTHER WAYS OF SAYING *How much did your bike cost?*
> *How much did you pay for your bike?*
> *What was the price of your bike?*
> *How much is your bike worth?*

costume *noun*
We had to wear special costumes for the play.
  ▶ **clothes   a disguise   fancy dress   an outfit**

cosy *adjective*
The room was small and cosy.
  ▶ **comfortable   snug   warm**

count *verb*
She counted the money.
  ▶ **to add up**

country *noun*
1 *Australia is a big country.*
  ▶ **a land   a nation**
  a kingdom (*a country with a king or queen*)
2 *Do you live in the country or in a town?*
  ▶ **the countryside**

courage *noun*
We were all impressed with his courage.
  ▶ **bravery   heroism   valour**

a
b
c
d
e
f
g
h
i
j
k
l
m
n
o
p
q
r
s
t
u
v
w
x
y
z

cover *noun*
1 *She put a cover over the dish.*
► a lid   a top   a covering
2 *He threw a cover over the sleeping baby.*
► a blanket   a duvet

cover *verb*
1 *She covered him with a blanket.*
► to wrap someone in *She wrapped him in a blanket.*
2 *He pulled his sleeve down to cover the scar on his arm.*
► to hide   to conceal

coward *noun*
He's a real coward!
► a wimp   a chicken

crack *noun*
1 *He handed me an old cup with a crack in it.*
► a break   a chip
2 *There was a crack in the wall.*
► a hole   a gap   a split

crack *verb*
Mind you don't crack the glass.
► to break   to chip   to smash   to shatter

crafty *adjective*
Foxes are crafty animals.
► clever   cunning   sly   sneaky   wily

crash *noun*
1 *There was a crash on the motorway.*
► an accident   a smash   a collision
a pile-up (*a crash with a lot of cars*)
2 *The tree fell down with a loud crash.*
► a bang   a thud   a clatter   a bump   a thump

crash *verb*

1 *The car crashed into a wall.*
   ▶ **to smash into   to bang into**
      to hit *The car hit a wall.*
2 *Two lorries crashed on the motorway.*
   ▶ **to collide   to have an accident**
3 *My computer has just crashed.*
   ▶ **to go down**

crawl *verb*
We crawled through the tunnel.
   ▶ **to creep   to climb   to slither   to wriggle**

crazy *adjective*

1 *Everyone thought he was just a crazy old man.*
   ▶ **mad   silly   stupid**
   ←→ An opposite is **sensible**.
2 *The children went crazy when they saw the clown.*
   ▶ **mad   berserk**

creak *verb*
The old door creaked as it opened.
   ▶ **to squeak   to scrape**

crease *verb*
Mind you don't crease your skirt.
   ▶ **to crumple   to crush**

creep *verb*

1 *We crept through a hole in the hedge.*
   ▶ **to crawl   to climb   to slither   to wriggle**
2 *He crept away when no one was looking.*
   ▶ **to sneak   to slip   to steal   to tiptoe**

crime *noun*
You have committed a terrible crime.
   ▶ **an offence   a sin**

criminal *noun*
These criminals must be caught.
   ▶ **a crook   a villain   a wrongdoer   an outlaw** (*in the past*)
      a thief   a robber   a murderer   an offender

crisp *adjective*
She bit into the crisp toast.
- ▶ **crunchy hard**
- ←→ An opposite is **soft**.

criticize *verb*
1 You shouldn't criticize other people's work.
- ▶ **to find fault with** You shouldn't find fault with other people's work.
  to pick holes in You shouldn't pick holes in other people's work.
2 Stop criticizing me!
- ▶ **to get at** Stop getting at me!
  to put down Stop putting me down!
- ←→ An opposite is **praise**.

crooked *adjective*
1 We sat down by an old, crooked tree.
- ▶ **bent twisted misshapen**
2 They climbed up the crooked path.
- ▶ **winding twisting bendy**
- ←→ An opposite is **straight**.

cross *adjective*
My mum was really cross with me.
- ▶ **angry annoyed**
  furious (*very cross*)
  livid (*very cross indeed*)
  irritated (*slightly cross*)
- ←→ An opposite is **pleased**.

> **❝❞** OTHER WAYS OF SAYING *She got cross.*
> She lost her temper.
> She flew off the handle.
> She went mad.

cross *verb*
Take care when you cross the road.
- ▶ **to go across to go over**

cross out *verb*
I crossed out my name.
- ▶ **to erase to delete to rub out**

crouch verb
She crouched down to pick up a shell.
▶ to bend   to stoop   to squat

crowd noun
A crowd of people was waiting outside the cinema.
▶ a group   a mass   a horde
a mob (*a noisy crowd*)
a rabble (*a very noisy crowd*)

crowded adjective
The airport was very crowded.
▶ busy   full   packed   swarming with people
teeming with people
← → An opposite is **empty**.

cruel adjective
1 *The king was a cruel man.*
▶ wicked   unkind   heartless   brutal
2 *Some people think bullfighting is a cruel sport.*
▶ barbaric   inhumane
← → An opposite is **kind**.

crumb noun
All they had to eat was a few crumbs of bread.
▶ a bit   a scrap

crunch verb
He crunched his apple noisily.
▶ to chew   to munch   to chomp

crush verb
Mind you don't crush the flowers.
▶ to squash   to flatten   to damage   to break

cry verb
1 *Some of the children were crying.*
▶ to weep   to sob   to shed tears   to snivel   to blubber
2 *'Look out!' she cried.*
▶ to shout   to call   to yell   to scream   to shriek   to exclaim

a b c d e f g h i j k l m n o p q r s t u v w x y z

61

cuddle verb

She cuddled her little brother.

▶ to hug   to embrace   to hold

cunning adjective

He thought of a cunning plan to escape.

▶ clever   crafty   ingenious   sneaky

cup noun

••• SOME TYPES OF CUP

a beaker	a glass	a goblet
a mug	a teacup	a tumbler

cure verb

Doctors can cure this disease.

▶ to treat   to heal

curious adjective

1 *We were all very curious about the new teacher.*

▶ inquisitive   nosy

2 *There was a curious smell in the kitchen.*

▶ strange   funny   odd   peculiar

curtain noun

▶ a drape   a blind

curve noun

1 *There was a curve in the road ahead of us.*

▶ a bend   a turn

2 *We can make a pattern using straight lines and curves.*

▶ a loop   a curl   a swirl   an arc

custom noun

It's the custom to give someone presents on their birthday.

▶ a tradition

cut noun

She had a cut on her finger.

▶ a wound   a graze   a gash (*a big cut*)   a nick (*a small cut*)

cut *verb*

1 *I fell over and cut my knee.*
▶ **to graze   to wound   to gash** (*to cut badly*)
a nick (*a small cut*)

2 *Cut the meat into small pieces.*
▶ **to chop   to chop up   to slice**
to dice (*to cut into small square pieces*)
to mince (*to cut into tiny pieces*)

3 *I'll cut the bread.*
▶ **to slice**

4 *We cut some wood.*
▶ **to chop   to saw**

5 *The hairdresser cut my hair.*
▶ **to trim   to snip**

6 *We need to cut the grass.*
▶ **to mow**

7 *Dad cut the hedge.*
▶ **to prune   to trim   to clip**

cut off *verb*

He had an accident and cut off one of his fingers.
▶ **to chop off   to sever**
to amputate *Doctors had to amputate his leg because it was so badly injured.*

Dd

damage verb

1 *Mind you don't damage any of the books.*
▶ to spoil   to ruin

2 *She dropped the box and damaged some of the plates.*
▶ to break   to chip   to scratch   to smash

3 *The explosion damaged several buildings.*
▶ to destroy

4 *The crash damaged our car quite badly.*
▶ to wreck

5 *Smoking can damage your health.*
▶ to harm

damp adjective

The grass was rather damp.
▶ wet   moist
←→ An opposite is **dry**.

dance verb

1 *Everyone was dancing to the music.*
▶ to jig about   to leap about

2 *The children were all dancing about with excitement.*
▶ to skip about   to jump about   to leap about
to prance about

dance noun

1 *He did a little dance.*
▶ a jig

● ● ● **SOME TYPES OF DANCE**

ballet	the cancan	country dancing
disco	Irish dancing	the jive
line dancing	rock and roll	Scottish dancing
the tango	the waltz	

---

2 *They were all invited to a dance at the palace.*
▶ a party   a ball   a disco

danger *noun*

1 *The animals could sense danger.*
▶ trouble

2 *There is a danger that you might fall.*
▶ a risk   a chance   a possibility

dangerous *adjective*

1 *It is dangerous to play with matches.*
▶ risky   unsafe
← → An opposite is **safe**.

> 66 99 **OTHER WAYS OF SAYING** *This is dangerous.*
> *You might get hurt.*
> *You might get killed.*
> *You are in danger.*
> *You are risking your life.*

2 *A knife is a dangerous weapon.*
▶ lethal   deadly

3 *The factory produces some very dangerous chemicals.*
▶ poisonous   toxic   hazardous

4 *This man is a dangerous criminal.*
▶ violent

dare *verb*

1 *Come and catch me, if you dare!*
▶ to be brave enough   to have the courage
to have the nerve

2 *I dare you to climb that tree.*
▶ to challenge

daring *adjective*

Which of you boys is the most daring?
▶ brave   bold   courageous   fearless   adventurous
← → An opposite is **timid**.

a
b
c
d
e
f
g
h
i
j
k
l
m
n
o
p
q
r
s
t
u
v
w
x
y
z

dark *adjective*

1 *It was dark outside.*
  ▶ black   pitch-black
  ←→ An opposite is **light**.

2 *He was left alone in a dark room.*
  ▶ gloomy   dingy   unlit
  ←→ An opposite is **bright**.

3 *They walked through the dark woods.*
  ▶ shady   shadowy   gloomy
  ←→ An opposite is **bright**.

4 *She has dark hair.*
  ▶ black   brown   ebony (*very dark*)   jet black (*very dark*)
  ←→ An opposite is **light**.

darling *noun*
Take care, darling.
  ▶ dear   love   sweetheart

dash *verb*
She dashed out of the room.
  ▶ to run   to rush   to sprint   to fly   to dart   to hurry

dawdle *verb*
They dawdled along.
  ▶ to stroll   to amble   to wander

dead *adjective*

1 *My grandmother is dead now.*
  ▶ gone   deceased   no longer alive
  passed away *My grandmother has passed away.*

2 *We found the dead body of a fox.*
  ▶ lifeless

deadly *adjective*
This poison is deadly.
  ▶ dangerous   lethal   fatal
  ←→ An opposite is **harmless**.

deal out *verb*
You deal out the cards.
  ▶ to give out   to hand out   to share out   to distribute

deal with *verb*
I will deal with this problem.
▶ to handle   to sort out   to cope with

dear *adjective*
1 He was delighted to see his dear daughter again.
▶ beloved   darling
2 Those trainers are very dear.
▶ expensive   costly
← → An opposite is **cheap**.

deceive *verb*
He tried to deceive us.
▶ to trick   to mislead   to fool

decent *adjective*
I want to watch a decent film for once.
▶ good   proper

decide *verb*
1 He decided to tell his parents everything.
▶ to make up your mind *He made up his mind to tell his parents everything.*
to resolve *He resolved to tell his parents everything.*
2 I can't decide which cake to have.
▶ to choose

decorate *verb*
1 They decorated the Christmas tree with tinsel.
▶ to adorn   to beautify
2 This summer we need to decorate your bedroom.
▶ to paint   to wallpaper

deep *adjective*
The treasure was hidden at the bottom of a deep hole.
▶ bottomless (*very deep*)
← → An opposite is **shallow**.

defeat

defeat *verb*

1 *They finally defeated their enemies.*
  ▶ to beat to overcome to conquer

2 *We defeated the other team quite easily.*
  ▶ to beat
  to thrash (*to defeat by a lot of points*)

defend *verb*

We must stay and defend the city.
  ▶ to protect to guard
  to keep safe *We must stay and keep the city safe.*

definite *adjective*

1 *The party will probably be next Saturday, but it's not definite yet.*
  ▶ certain fixed settled

2 *I can see a definite improvement in your work.*
  ▶ clear obvious positive

delay *verb*

1 *The bad weather delayed us.*
  ▶ to hold someone up *The bad weather held us up.*
  to slow someone down *The bad weather slowed us down.*
  to make someone late *The bad weather made us late.*

2 *We had to delay the start of the race.*
  ▶ to postpone to put off

deliberate *adjective*

He said it was a deliberate mistake.
  ▶ intentional planned
  ←→ An opposite is **accidental**.

deliberately *adverb*

She deliberately left the gate open.
  ▶ on purpose intentionally knowingly
  ←→ An opposite is **accidentally**.

delicate *adjective*

A lot of the objects in the museum are very old and delicate.
  ▶ fragile flimsy

delicious *adjective*
This food is delicious!
▶ lovely tasty scrumptious gorgeous
← → An opposite is **horrible**.

delighted *adjective*
I was delighted with your present.
▶ pleased thrilled overjoyed ecstatic

deliver *verb*
We will deliver the new computer to your house.
▶ to bring to take

demand *verb*
She demanded an explanation.
▶ to insist on to ask for to request

demolish *verb*
They are going to demolish the old school building.
▶ to knock down to pull down to bulldoze to flatten

deny *verb*
She denied that she had stolen the money.
▶ to refuse to admit *She refused to admit that she had stolen the money.*
← → An opposite is **admit**.

depend on *verb*
The young chicks depend on their mother for food.
▶ to need to rely on

depressed *adjective*
He was feeling depressed.
▶ sad unhappy upset low dejected

describe *verb*
1 *She described the animal she had seen.*
▶ to give a description of *She gave a description of the animal.*
2 *The boy described how he had escaped.*
▶ to explain to relate to recount to report

a
b
c
d
e
f
g
h
i
j
k
l
m
n
o
p
q
r
s
t
u
v
w
x
y
z

deserted *adjective*
They walked through the deserted village.
▶ empty   abandoned

design *verb*
They have designed a new type of engine.
▶ to create   to make   to invent   to devise   to plan

desperate *adjective*
I was desperate for a drink.
▶ dying for

destroy *verb*
1 *The explosion destroyed several buildings.*
▶ to demolish   to flatten
2 *The fire destroyed many valuable old books.*
▶ to ruin

determined *adjective*
1 *We are determined to win.*
▶ resolved   single-minded   obstinate
2 *You have to be very determined if you want to succeed.*
▶ single-minded   strong-willed

develop *verb*
Tadpoles gradually develop into frogs.
▶ to change into   to grow into   to evolve into

device *noun*
They use a special device for opening the bottles.
▶ a gadget   a tool   an implement

diagram *noun*
We drew a diagram of the machine.
▶ a plan   a drawing   a sketch

diary *noun*
I am keeping a diary of our holiday.
▶ a journal   a daily record

die *verb*

1 *My grandfather died last year.*
  ▶ to pass away

2 *Hundreds of people died in the fire.*
  ▶ to perish
    to be killed *Hundreds of people were killed in the fire.*

3 *The plants died because I forgot to water them.*
  ▶ to dry up   to shrivel   to wither

difference *noun*

Can you see any differences between the two pictures?
  ▶ a discrepancy   an inconsistency   a variation
  ← → An opposite is **similarity**.

different *adjective*

1 *Your book is different to mine.*
  ▶ dissimilar   unlike
  ← → An opposite is **similar**.

> ❝ ❞ OTHER WAYS OF SAYING *Your book is different to mine.*
> *Your book is not like mine.*
> *Your book is not the same as mine.*

2 *Our ice cream is available in five different flavours.*
  ▶ assorted   various

3 *Each one of the puppies is slightly different.*
  ▶ special   distinctive   individual
    unique (*not like any others*)

4 *Let's do something different for a change!*
  ▶ new   exciting   unusual   extraordinary

5 *Our new neighbours are certainly different!*
  ▶ strange   peculiar   odd   unusual   bizarre

difficult *adjective*

The teacher gave us some very difficult work to do.
  ▶ hard   tough   tricky   complicated
  ← → An opposite is **easy**.

a
b
c
d
e
f
g
h
i
j
k
l
m
n
o
p
q
r
s
t
u
v
w
x
y
z

difficulty noun
We have had a few difficulties.
▶ **a problem   a snag** (*a small difficulty*)

dig verb
1 *We dug a hole in the garden.*
▶ **to make   to excavate**
2 *We dug down to find the treasure.*
▶ **to burrow   to tunnel**

dim adjective
A dim light was shining in the window.
▶ **faint   dull   pale**
← → An opposite is **bright**.

dip verb
She dipped her hand into the water.
▶ **to lower   to drop   to plunge   to immerse**

dirt noun
Their clothes were covered in dirt.
▶ **mud   muck   dust   grime   filth**

dirty adjective
1 *Why are your clothes so dirty?*
▶ **muddy   mucky   grubby   filthy   grimy**
2 *The room was very dirty.*
▶ **dusty   messy   filthy**
3 *The water in some rivers is very dirty.*
▶ **polluted   foul**
← → An opposite is **clean**.

disagree verb
The two boys always seem to disagree about everything.
▶ **to argue   to quarrel   to have different opinions**
← → An opposite is **agree**.

disappear *verb*
The dog disappeared into some bushes.
▶ to vanish
←→ An opposite is **appear**.

disappointed *adjective*
I was very disappointed when the trip was cancelled.
▶ upset sad dejected downcast

disaster *noun*
The plane crash was a terrible disaster.
▶ a tragedy a catastrophe a calamity

discover *verb*
1 *Who first discovered electricity?*
▶ to find out about *Who first found out about electricity?*
to invent
2 *We have discovered a lot about dinosaurs.*
▶ to find out to learn
3 *We discovered an old map in the attic.*
▶ to find to come across to uncover to unearth

discuss *verb*
We will discuss this later.
▶ to talk about to debate

discussion *noun*
We had a discussion about different religions.
▶ a talk a conversation a chat

disease *noun*
Quite a lot of children suffer from this disease.
▶ an illness a complaint a sickness an infection

disgusting *adjective*
This food is disgusting!
▶ horrible revolting foul
←→ An opposite is **lovely**.

a
b
c
d
e
f
g
h
i
j
k
l
m
n
o
p
q
r
s
t
u
v
w
x
y
z

a
b
c
d
e
f
g
h
i
j
k
l
m
n
o
p
q
r
s
t
u
v
w
x
y
z

dish *noun*
She put the vegetables in a dish.
▶ a bowl   a plate   a platter

display *noun*
We made a display of our paintings.
▶ an exhibition   a presentation

display *verb*
We will display the best pictures in the hall.
▶ to show   to hang up   to exhibit

distance *noun*
We measured the distance between the two posts.
▶ the space   the gap   the length   the width

distant *adjective*
They travelled to many distant lands.
▶ faraway   far off   remote

distinguish *verb*
Can you distinguish skimmed milk from semi-skimmed?
▶ to differentiate   to tell apart

disturb *verb*
1 *I'm working, so please don't disturb me.*
▶ to interrupt   to pester   to bother
2 *The sight of so many soldiers disturbed me.*
▶ to worry   to trouble   to alarm   to distress

dive *verb*
She dived into the water.
▶ to plunge   to leap   to jump

divide *verb*
1 *We can divide the sweets between us.*
▶ to share   to split
2 *She divided the cake into ten pieces.*
▶ to cut   to split   to separate

dizzy *adjective*
I felt weak and dizzy.
▶ **giddy faint light-headed unsteady**

do *verb*
1 *What are you doing?*
   ▶ **to be up to** *What are you up to?*
2 *They are in danger—we must do something!*
   ▶ **to take action to act**
3 *I usually try to do my work quickly.*
   ▶ **to get on with**
4 *Dad does our breakfast at the weekends.*
   ▶ **to prepare to cook**
5 *We're going to do an experiment.*
   ▶ **to carry out to conduct**
6 *I can't do this sum.*
   ▶ **to work out to calculate**
7 *Have you done all your homework?*
   ▶ **to finish to complete**
8 *You have done very well.*
   ▶ **to get on to perform**

doctor *noun*

●●● SOME TYPES OF DOCTOR
a **general practitioner**
a **G.P.**
a **consultant** (*a doctor in a hospital*)
a **specialist** (*a doctor who knows a lot about one type of illness*)
a **surgeon** (*a doctor who performs operations*)
a **paediatrician** (*a doctor who looks after children*)
a **physiotherapist** (*a doctor who helps people use their muscles again after an illness or an injury*)
an **optician** (*a doctor who checks your eyes*)

---

a
b
c
d
e
f
g
h
i
j
k
l
m
n
o
p
q
r
s
t
u
v
w
x
y
z

a
b
c
d
e
f
g
h
i
j
k
l
m
n
o
p
q
r
s
t
u
v
w
x
y
z

dog noun

> *Focus on* **dog**
>
> ► **a hound   a bitch** (*a female dog*)
>   **a puppy** (*a young dog*)
>   **a mongrel** (*a dog that is a mixture of breeds*)
>
> SOME TYPES OF DOG
> | | | |
> |---|---|---|
> | **an Alsatian** | **a beagle** | **a boxer** |
> | **a bulldog** | **a chihuahua** | **a collie** |
> | **a dachshund** | **a Dalmatian** | **a Great Dane** |
> | **a greyhound** | **a Labrador** | **a poodle** |
> | **a retriever** | **a sheepdog** | **a spaniel** |
> | **a terrier** | | |
>
> SOME WORDS YOU MIGHT USE TO DESCRIBE THE SOUNDS
> A DOG MAKES
> | | | |
> |---|---|---|
> | **to bark** | **to yap** | **to growl** |
> | **to snarl** | **to whine** | **to yelp** |
> | **to pant** | | |

dot noun
There were red dots all over the wall.
► **a spot   a mark   a speck**

doubt noun
There's some doubt about whether she will be well enough to play.
► **concern   worry   anxiety   uncertainty**

doubt verb
I doubt whether she'll be well enough to sing in the concert.
► **to question   to wonder   to be uncertain about**

drag verb
We dragged the box out into the hall.
► **to pull   to haul   to lug**

draw verb
1 *Can you draw a picture of a house?*
► **to sketch   to paint   to trace**
2 *She drew the curtains.*
► **to close   to open   to pull back**
3 *The two teams drew in the last game.*
► **to finish equal   to tie**

dreadful *adjective*
The whole house was in a dreadful mess.
▶ terrible awful appalling

dream *noun*
1 Do you ever remember your dreams?
▶ a bad dream (*a horrible dream*)
a nightmare (*a frightening dream*)
2 Her dream is to be a famous ballet dancer.
▶ an ambition a wish a goal

dress *noun*
She was wearing a red dress.
▶ a frock a gown (*a long, smart dress*)

dress *verb*
1 Hurry up and get dressed.
▶ to put clothes on
2 He was dressed in a black suit.
▶ to be attired in *He was attired in a black suit.*
to be wearing *He was wearing a black suit.*
to have on *He had a black suit on.*

drift *verb*
The little boat drifted out to sea.
▶ to float to be carried

drink *verb*
1 If you are thirsty, you need to drink.
▶ to quench your thirst
2 He drank his milk quickly.
▶ to gulp down to swig to knock back to swallow
3 She drank her wine slowly.
▶ to sip
4 The dog drank its water.
▶ to lap up

drip *verb*
Water was dripping from the trees above us.
▶ to drop to splash to trickle to dribble

drive *verb*

1 *She got into her car and drove off.*
▶ **to speed   to zoom   to crawl** (*to drive slowly*)

2 *She drove the car into the parking space.*
▶ **to steer   to guide   to manoeuvre**

3 *We decided to drive to London rather than going by train.*
▶ **to go by car**

droop *verb*

The flowers were beginning to droop.
▶ **to wilt   to flop**

drop *noun*

I felt a few drops of rain on my face.
▶ **a drip   a spot   a droplet**

drop *verb*

He accidentally dropped his glass.
▶ **to let go of**

> **"** ANOTHER WAY OF SAYING *He dropped his glass.*
> *The glass slipped out of his hand.*

dry *adjective*

1 *The ground was very dry.*
▶ **hard   parched   arid**
← → An opposite is **wet**.

2 *They lived on dry bread and water.*
▶ **hard   stale**

duck *noun*

Focus on **duck**
▶ **a drake** (*a male duck*)   **a duckling** (*a young duck*)

SOME WORDS YOU MIGHT USE TO DESCRIBE HOW A DUCK
WALKS OR SWIMS
to waddle   to swim   to paddle
to dabble   to dive

A WORD YOU MIGHT USE TO DESCRIBE THE SOUND A DUCK
MAKES
to quack

dull *adjective*
1 *I think this television show is very dull.*
  ▶ boring tedious uninteresting
  ←→ An opposite is **interesting**.
2 *She was wearing a dull green dress.*
  ▶ drab dark dreary dowdy
  ←→ An opposite is **bright**.
3 *It was a rather dull day.*
  ▶ grey cloudy overcast dismal
  ←→ An opposite is **bright**.

dump *noun*
All the rubbish is taken to the rubbish dump.
  ▶ a tip a rubbish heap

dump *verb*
1 *Some people dump rubbish by the side of the road.*
  ▶ to leave to throw away to discard
2 *She dumped her bags on the kitchen floor.*
  ▶ to drop to throw to fling

dusty *adjective*
The room was very dusty.
  ▶ dirty filthy mucky
  ←→ An opposite is **clean**.

duty *noun*
It is your duty to look after the younger children.
  ▶ a responsibility a job

a b c d e f g h i j k l m n o p q r s t u v w x y z

a
b
c
d
e
f
g
h
i
j
k
l
m
n
o
p
q
r
s
t
u
v
w
x
y
z

Ee

eager *adjective*
We were eager to go out and play.
▶ keen impatient anxious
←→ An opposite is **reluctant**.

earn *verb*
You can earn money by delivering newspapers.
▶ to make to get

earth *noun*
1 *This is the largest lake on earth.*
▶ the world the globe the planet
2 *Bulbs will start to grow when you plant them in the earth.*
▶ soil ground

easy *adjective*
These sums are easy.
▶ simple straightforward not difficult
←→ An opposite is **difficult**.

eat *verb*
1 *What time do you usually eat your lunch?*
▶ to have
2 *Someone has eaten all the cake.*
▶ to guzzle to polish off to scoff
3 *He quickly ate his toast and ran out.*
▶ to wolf down to bolt to gobble
4 *She was eating an apple.*
▶ to munch to crunch to chomp
5 *The children were eating sweets.*
▶ to chew to suck
6 *The rabbit was eating a lettuce leaf.*
▶ to nibble to bite
7 *The lion ate its prey.*
▶ to devour

edge *noun*

1 *I bumped my leg on the edge of the table.*
▶ **the side**

2 *There was a pattern around the edge of the plate.*
▶ **the outside**

3 *The edge of the cup was cracked.*
▶ **the rim**

4 *We walked right to the edge of the field.*
▶ **the boundary**

5 *Keep close to the edge of the road when you are walking.*
▶ **the side   the verge   the kerb**

6 *We live on the edge of the town.*
▶ **the outskirts   the suburbs**

effect *noun*

What will be the effect of the hot sun on these plants?
▶ **result   impact   consequence**

effort *noun*

1 *You should put more effort into your spellings.*
▶ **work**

> **❝❞** OTHER WAYS OF SAYING *You should put more effort in.*
> *You should try harder.*
> *You should work harder.*

2 *I made an effort to be cheerful.*
▶ **an attempt**

> **❝❞** OTHER WAYS OF SAYING *I made an effort.*
> *I tried.*
> *I did my best.*
> *I had a go.*

elect *verb*

We elect a new school captain each year.
▶ **to choose   to pick   to vote for   to appoint**

embarrassed *adjective*

I felt really embarrassed.
▶ **uncomfortable   awkward   ashamed   shy   self-conscious**

emergency *noun*

Be quick, it's an emergency!
▶ a crisis

> ❝ **OTHER WAYS OF SAYING** *It's an emergency.*
> *It's urgent.*
> *It's a matter of life and death.*

empty *adjective*

1 *There was an empty lemonade bottle on the table.*
▶ **unfilled**
←→ An opposite is **full**.

2 *They've moved away, so their house is empty.*
▶ **unoccupied bare unfurnished**
←→ An opposite is **occupied**.

3 *It was raining, so the town centre was empty.*
▶ **deserted**
←→ An opposite is **crowded**.

encourage *verb*

1 *My parents encouraged me to learn the violin.*
▶ **to persuade to urge**

2 *We all cheered to encourage our team.*
▶ **to support to cheer on to inspire**
←→ An opposite is **discourage**.

end *noun*

1 *We walked right to the end of the lane.*
▶ **the limit the boundary**

2 *Please go to the end of the queue.*
▶ **the back the rear**

3 *He tied a balloon to the end of the stick.*
▶ **the tip the top the bottom**

4 *I didn't like the end of the film.*
▶ **the ending the close**

5 *This book has a happy end.*
▶ **an ending a conclusion a resolution**

end verb

1 *When will the concert end?*
▶ to stop   to finish

2 *Will this rain ever end?*
▶ to stop   to cease

3 *How does the film end?*
▶ to finish   to conclude

enemy noun

He fought bravely against his enemy.
▶ an opponent   a foe   a rival
← → An opposite is **friend**.

energetic adjective

I'm feeling quite energetic this morning.
▶ active   lively   full of beans
   hyperactive (*very energetic*)

energy noun

The children seem to have a lot of energy today.
▶ strength   stamina

enjoy verb

I really enjoyed that book.
▶ to like   to love   to take pleasure from

enjoyable adjective

It was a very enjoyable trip.
▶ pleasant   pleasurable   delightful
← → An opposite is **unpleasant**.

enough adjective

Have you got enough money to buy an ice cream?
▶ sufficient

enter verb

1 *She entered the room.*
▶ to go into   to come into   to walk into   to run into
← → An opposite is **leave**.

2 *Are you going to enter the competition?*
▶ to go in for   to take part in   to join in

entertain *verb*
The clown entertained the children.
▶ to amuse
to make someone laugh *The clown made the children laugh.*

enthusiastic *adjective*
He is very enthusiastic about joining the football team.
▶ keen *He is keen to join the football team.*
eager *He is eager to join the football team.*

entrance *noun*
1 *We couldn't find the entrance to the building.*
▶ the way in   the door   the gate
← → An opposite is **exit**.
2 *They stood by the entrance to the cave.*
▶ the mouth   the opening

equal *adjective*
The two teams have an equal number of points.
▶ identical

equipment *noun*
We keep the games equipment in the shed.
▶ things   gear   tackle   apparatus

escape *verb*
1 *The robbers escaped from prison.*
▶ to get away   to run away
to make your escape *The robbers made their escape.*
2 *The soldiers chased us but we managed to escape.*
▶ to get away
to give someone the slip *We managed to give them the slip.*
3 *We went indoors to escape from the rain.*
▶ to avoid

estimate *noun*
What is your estimate of how tall you are?
▶ a calculation   a guess

estimate *verb*
I estimate that it will take us two hours to get there.
▶ to guess   to calculate   to reckon

even *adjective*

1 *You need an even surface for cycling.*
▶ flat smooth level
←→ An opposite is **uneven**.

2 *Their scores were even at half time.*
▶ equal level the same
←→ An opposite is **different**.

evening *noun*
We should be there by evening.
▶ dusk nightfall sunset

event *noun*

1 *The party will be a big event.*
▶ an occasion

2 *Some strange events have been happening.*
▶ an incident

eventually *adverb*
We got home eventually.
▶ finally at last in the end

evidence *noun*
Where is your evidence for this idea?
▶ proof facts information

evil *adjective*

1 *This was an evil deed.*
▶ wicked cruel vile

2 *An evil king ruled over the land.*
▶ wicked bad cruel black-hearted
←→ An opposite is **good**.

exact *adjective*
Make sure you add the exact amount of water.
▶ right correct precise

exam *noun*
We've got a maths exam tomorrow.
▶ a test an examination

a
b
c
d
e
f
g
h
i
j
k
l
m
n
o
p
q
r
s
t
u
v
w
x
y
z

example noun
Can you show us an example of your work?
▶ a sample   a specimen

excellent adjective
This is an excellent piece of work.
▶ very good   wonderful   brilliant   first-class   superb
outstanding
← → An opposite is **bad**.

exchange verb
I exchanged my old bike for a new one.
▶ to change   to swap

excited adjective
She was very excited because it was her birthday.
▶ happy   thrilled   enthusiastic
← → An opposite is **calm**.

excitement noun
I like films with a lot of excitement.
▶ action   drama   suspense

exciting adjective
1 *It was a very exciting film.*
▶ thrilling   gripping   action-packed
2 *Waterskiing is a very exciting sport.*
▶ exhilarating   thrilling
3 *It was a very exciting game to watch.*
▶ fast-moving   tense   nail-biting
4 *We had a very exciting day.*
▶ eventful   enjoyable
← → An opposite is **boring**.

excuse verb
Please excuse me for being late.
▶ to forgive   to pardon

exercise noun
You should do more exercise.
▶ sport   PE   games   running around

exhausted *adjective*
I was exhausted after my long walk.
▶ **tired   worn out   shattered**

exhibition *noun*
We made an exhibition of our paintings.
▶ **a display**

exist *verb*
Dragons don't really exist.
▶ **to live**

> 6 9 **OTHER WAYS OF SAYING** *Dragons don't really exist.*
> *There are no dragons.*
> *There are no such things as dragons.*

exit *noun*
Where is the exit?
▶ **the way out   the door**

expect *verb*
I expect it will rain later.
▶ **to think   to believe   to suppose**

expensive *adjective*
Those trousers are very expensive.
▶ **dear   costly**
← → An opposite is **cheap**.

explain *verb*
He explained how the machine worked.
▶ **to describe**
to show *He showed us how the machine worked.*

explode *verb*
1 *The firework exploded with a shower of stars.*
▶ **to go off   to burst   to go bang**
2 *The car caught fire and exploded.*
▶ **to blow up**

a
b
c
d
e
f
g
h
i
j
k
l
m
n
o
p
q
r
s
t
u
v
w
x
y
z

explore verb
Let's explore the cave.
▶ to look round   to search   to investigate

expression noun
He had a sad expression on his face.
▶ a look

> 66 99 OTHER WAYS OF SAYING He had a sad expression on
> his face.
> He looked sad.
> His face was sad.
> He had a sad appearance.

extra adjective
I've brought some extra food in case we get hungry.
▶ more   additional

extraordinary adjective
Standing before us was an extraordinary creature.
▶ strange   bizarre   incredible   remarkable   unusual
amazing
←→ An opposite is **ordinary**.

extreme adjective
No plants can grow in the extreme heat of the desert.
▶ great   intense   severe

extremely adverb
You are extremely lucky.
▶ very   incredibly   exceptionally   unbelievably

face noun
The little boy had a sad face.
▶ an expression

fact noun
We found out some interesting facts about the ancient Romans.
▶ **information** We found out some interesting information about the Romans.
data We have been collecting data on the ancient Romans.

fade verb
1 The colour in my dress has faded.
▶ to become lighter
2 It was evening, and the light was beginning to fade.
▶ to go to dwindle
3 The sound of the engine gradually faded.
▶ to become faint to disappear

failure noun
The magician's trick was a complete failure!
▶ a disaster a flop
← → An opposite is **success**.

faint adjective
1 I heard a faint cry.
▶ quiet weak muffled dim
← → An opposite is **loud**.
2 The writing was quite faint and difficult to read.
▶ unclear indistinct
← → An opposite is **clear**.

faint verb
I fainted because it was so hot.
▶ to pass out to lose consciousness

a
b
c
d
e
f
g
h
i
j
k
l
m
n
o
p
q
r
s
t
u
v
w
x
y
z

fair *adjective*

1 *Tom has fair hair.*
▶ **blond** (*for a boy*) **blonde** (*for a girl*) **light** **golden**
←→ An opposite is **dark**.

2 *It's not fair if she gets more sweets than me.*
▶ **right**
←→ An opposite is **unfair**.

3 *I don't think the referee was very fair.*
▶ **impartial unbiased honest**
←→ An opposite is **biased**.

4 *We've got a fair chance of winning.*
▶ **reasonable good moderate decent**

faithful *adjective*
Joshua was his faithful friend.
▶ **loyal devoted**
←→ An opposite is **unfaithful**.

fake *noun*
He knew that the painting was a fake.
▶ **a forgery a copy**

fall *verb*

1 *Mind you don't fall.*
▶ **to trip to slip to stumble to lose your balance**

2 *He fell off his chair.*
▶ **to tumble to slip**

3 *She tripped and fell into the river.*
▶ **to plunge**

4 *The book fell to the floor.*
▶ **to drop to tumble**
 to crash (*to fall with a loud noise*)

5 *Snow began to fall.*
▶ **to come down**

fall down *verb*
The old school fell down a few years ago.
▶ **to collapse**

false *adjective*

1 *He was wearing a false beard.*
  ▶ **fake artificial pretend**
  ←→ An opposite is **real**.

2 *He gave the police false information.*
  ▶ **incorrect misleading**
  ←→ An opposite is **correct**.

family *noun*

I really enjoy being with my family in the holidays.
  ▶ **relatives relations**

famous *adjective*

One day she might be a famous pop star.
  ▶ **well-known world-famous celebrated**
  ←→ An opposite is **unknown**.

fan *noun*

1 *I am a great fan of his.*
  ▶ **an admirer**

2 *My brother is a Manchester United fan.*
  ▶ **a supporter a follower**

fantastic *adjective*

We had a fantastic time.
  ▶ **wonderful brilliant great fabulous marvellous
  sensational**
  ←→ An opposite is **terrible**.

farm *noun*

●●● SOME TYPES OF FARM
  an arable farm (*one that grows crops*)
  a dairy farm (*one that keeps cows for milk*)
  a fruit farm
  a poultry farm (*one with chickens, ducks, or turkeys*)
  a ranch (*a cattle farm in North America*)
  a smallholding (*a small farm*)

a b c d e f g h i j k l m n o p q r s t u v w x y z

a
b
c
d
e
f
g
h
i
j
k
l
m
n
o
p
q
r
s
t
u
v
w
x
y
z

fashion *noun*
> *These shoes are the latest fashions.*
> ▸ a style   a trend   a craze   a look

fashionable *adjective*
> **1** *He wears very fashionable clothes.*
> ▸ trendy   stylish
> **2** *These coats are fashionable at the moment.*
> ▸ popular   in fashion   all the rage
> ← → An opposite is **unfashionable**.

fast *adjective*
> **1** *My dad's car is quite fast.*
> ▸ speedy   powerful
> **2** *We'll go on the fast train.*
> ▸ high-speed   express
> **3** *Scientists are working on a new fast aeroplane.*
> ▸ supersonic *(faster than the speed of sound)*
> **4** *He's a very fast runner.*
> ▸ quick   speedy
> **5** *We were walking at quite a fast pace.*
> ▸ brisk   quick   swift
> ← → An opposite is **slow**.

fasten *verb*
> **1** *Fasten your seatbelt.*
> ▸ to do up   to buckle
> **2** *I stopped to fasten my shoelaces.*
> ▸ to tie up   to do up
> **3** *Fasten the two bits of string together.*
> ▸ to tie   to fix   to join
> **4** *We fastened the boat to a post.*
> ▸ to tie   to secure

fat *adjective*
> **1** *The ticket collector was a little fat man.*
> ▸ stout   tubby   round   pot-bellied   portly
> **2** *Sometimes my brother worries that he is fat.*
> ▸ overweight   obese

▸▸

3 *On her knee was a fat, cuddly baby.*
▶ **plump   chubby   podgy**
←→ An opposite is **thin**.

fault *noun*

1 *The heating system has a fault, but we are trying to fix it.*
▶ **a problem   a defect   a malfunction**

2 *It's your fault that we're late.*

> ❝❞ OTHER WAYS OF SAYING *It's your fault.*
> *You are responsible.*
> *You caused it.*
> *You are to blame.*

favour *noun*

Please will you do me a favour?
▶ **a good turn**

> ❝❞ OTHER WAYS OF SAYING *Will you do me a favour?*
> *Will you do something for me?*
> *Will you help me?*

favourite *adjective*

What is your favourite book?
▶ **best-loved   number-one**

> ❝❞ ANOTHER WAY OF SAYING *This one is my favourite.*
> *I like this one best.*

fear *noun*

1 *I could see fear in his eyes.*
▶ **terror   panic**

2 *I have a terrible fear of snakes.*
▶ **a dread   a terror   a horror**

feel *verb*

She put out her hand and felt the puppy's fur.
▶ **to touch   to stroke**

a
b
c
d
e
f
g
h
i
j
k
l
m
n
o
p
q
r
s
t
u
v
w
x
y
z

feeling *noun*
Try to think about other people's feelings.
▶ an emotion

fence *noun*
There was a high fence around the garden.
▶ a railing   a wall

festival *noun*
Diwali is a Hindu religious festival.
▶ a celebration

fetch *verb*
1 Shall I fetch your bag for you?
▶ to get   to bring
2 I'll come and fetch you at five o'clock.
▶ to collect   to pick up

fiction *noun*
I like to read fiction.
▶ stories   tales   myths   legends   fantasies

field *noun*
1 We went for a walk through the fields.
▶ a meadow
2 The ponies have their own field behind the house.
▶ a paddock   an enclosure

fierce *adjective*
Tigers are very fierce animals.
▶ ferocious   savage   aggressive

fight *verb*
1 I don't like watching people fight.
▶ to brawl   to wrestle   to have a fight
2 Why are you two children always fighting.
▶ to argue   to quarrel   to bicker

fight *noun*
1 *The two boys had a fight after school.*
   ▶ a brawl   a punch-up
2 *There was a fight between two rival gangs.*
   ▶ a battle   a clash

fill *verb*
1 *We filled the boxes with toys.*
   ▶ to pack   to load   to stuff   to cram
2 *The men filled the lorry with crates.*
   ▶ to load
3 *They filled the huge balloon with air.*
   ▶ to inflate
← → An opposite is **empty**.

film *noun*
We watched a film on TV last night.
   ▶ a movie

●●● SOME TYPES OF FILM
   an adventure film
   a cartoon
   a documentary (*a film that gives you information about something*)
   a western (*a film about cowboys*)

---

filthy *adjective*
1 *The footballers were filthy by the end of the game.*
   ▶ dirty   muddy   mucky   grubby   grimy
2 *The room was filthy.*
   ▶ dirty   dusty   messy
3 *The water in this river is filthy.*
   ▶ polluted
← → An opposite is **clean**.

final

b
c
d
e
f
g
h
i
j
k
l
m
n
o
p
q
r
s
t
u
v
w
x
y
z

final *adjective*
This is the final day of the holidays.
▶ **last**

finally *adverb*
We finally arrived home at seven o'clock.
▶ **eventually   at last**

find *verb*
1 I can't find my homework.
▶ **to locate**
← → An opposite is **lose**.

> ❝ ❞ OTHER WAYS OF SAYING *I can't find my homework.*
> *I've lost my homework.*
> *My homework has gone missing.*

2 The children found an old map in the attic.
▶ **to discover   to come across   to stumble upon**
3 It took the police six months to find the missing man.
▶ **to trace   to track down**
4 When the archaeologists started digging, they found some very interesting things.
▶ **to dig up   to uncover   to unearth**

fine *adjective*
1 You will need to use a very fine thread.
▶ **thin   delicate**
← → An opposite is **thick**.
2 I hope the weather is fine for sports day.
▶ **sunny   dry   bright   clear   cloudless**
← → An opposite is **dull**.
3 I felt ill yesterday, but today I feel fine.
▶ **okay   all right**
← → An opposite is **ill**.

finish *verb*
1 What time does the film finish?
▶ **to end   to stop**
2 Have you finished your homework?
▶ **to complete   to do**

3 *Hurry up and finish your meal.*
  ▶ to eat   to eat up
4 *I haven't finished my drink.*
  ▶ to drink   to drink up
← → An opposite is **start**.

fire *noun*

1 *We lit a fire to keep us warm.*
  ▶ a bonfire (*a fire outside*)
2 *The explosion caused a huge fire.*
  ▶ a blaze   an inferno

fire *verb*

They were firing at a row of bottles on the wall.
  ▶ to shoot

firm *adjective*

1 *The ladder didn't feel very firm.*
  ▶ stable   secure   steady
  ← → An opposite is **unsteady**.
2 *We patted the sand down until it was firm.*
  ▶ hard
  ← → An opposite is **soft**.

first *adjective*

1 *We were the first to arrive.*
  ▶ earliest   soonest
2 *Who designed the first aeroplane?*
  ▶ earliest   original

fit *adjective*

1 *You have to be fit to play football.*
  ▶ strong   healthy
  ← → An opposite is **unfit**.
2 *I don't think this food is fit to eat.*
  ▶ suitable   good enough
  ← → An opposite is **unsuitable**.

a
b
c
d
e
f
g
h
i
j
k
l
m
n
o
p
q
r
s
t
u
v
w
x
y
z

fit *verb*

1 *These shoes fit me.*
▶ **to be the right size** *These shoes are the right size for me.*
2 *This box won't fit in the back of the car.*
▶ **to go**

fix *verb*

1 *Mum fixed the shelves onto the wall.*
▶ **to attach to tie to stick to nail to fasten**
2 *Our TV is broken and we can't fix it.*
▶ **to mend to repair**

fizzy *adjective*

She offered us a glass of fizzy lemonade.
▶ **sparkling bubbly**

flap *verb*

The loose sails were flapping in the wind.
▶ **to flutter to wave about**

flat *adjective*

You need a nice flat surface to work on.
▶ **level even smooth horizontal**
← → An opposite is **uneven**.

flavour *noun*

This drink has got a lovely flavour.
▶ **a taste**

flow *verb*

1 *A river flows through the town.*
▶ **to go to run to glide**
2 *The small stream flowed over the rocks.*
▶ **to gurgle to burble to babble**
3 *Water was flowing over the edge of the bath.*
▶ **to pour to stream to spill to gush to splash**
4 *Water was flowing out through cracks in the pipe.*
▶ **to leak to drip to trickle**

flower *noun*
1 *We admired the flowers on the rose bush.*
  ▶ a bloom
2 *The old apple tree has a lot of flowers on it this year.*
  ▶ blossom

● ● ●   SOME GARDEN FLOWERS

anemones	carnations	crocuses
daffodils	geraniums	lavender
lilac	lilies	marigolds
pansies	roses	snowdrops
sunflowers	sweet peas	tulips
wallflowers		

SOME WILD FLOWERS

bluebells	buttercups	daisies
dandelions	foxgloves	poppies
primroses		

---

fluffy *adjective*
She picked up the small, fluffy kitten.
  ▶ furry   soft   woolly

fly *verb*
1 *We watched the birds flying high above our heads.*
  ▶ to glide   to soar   to hover
2 *Small birds flew about among the trees.*
  ▶ to flutter   to flit   to dart
3 *The plane flew up into the sky.*
  ▶ to rise
4 *The eagle flew down onto its prey.*
  ▶ to swoop   to dive   to drop

fog *noun*
I couldn't see because of the fog.
  ▶ mist

follow

follow *verb*

1 *I ran off down the road, and the dog followed me.*
► to chase   to go after   to come after   to run after   to pursue

2 *I tried to follow them without being seen.*
► to shadow   to tail   to track

3 *Follow this road until you come to a crossroads.*
► to take   to go along   to continue along

4 *Follow my instructions carefully.*
► to pay attention to   to obey

food *noun*

1 *We were all tired and in need of food.*
► something to eat   refreshments   nourishment
grub (*informal*)   a meal

2 *We've got plenty of food for the animals.*
► feed   fodder

fool *noun*

Don't be such a fool!
► an idiot   a twit   an imbecile   a clown

fool *verb*

You can't fool me.
► to trick   to deceive

foolish *adjective*

That was a very foolish thing to do.
► silly   stupid   unwise
←→ An opposite is **sensible**.

foot *noun*

► a paw (*a dog's or cat's foot*)
a hoof (*a horse's foot*)
a trotter (*a pig's foot*)

force *noun*

1 *We had to use force to open the door.*
► strength

2 *The criminals used force to get into the building.*
► violence

a
b
c
d
e
f
g
h
i
j
k
l
m
n
o
p
q
r
s
t
u
v
w
x
y
z

force *verb*

1 *He forced me to give him money.*
  ▶ to **make** *He made me give him the money.*
    to **order** *He ordered me to give him the money.*
2 *They forced the door open.*
  ▶ to **push** to **break** to **smash**

forest *noun*

Don't get lost in the forest!
  ▶ a **wood** a **jungle** (*a tropical forest*)

forget *verb*

1 *I've forgotten his name.*

> **" "** OTHER WAYS OF SAYING *I've forgotten it.*
> *I can't remember it.*
> *It has slipped my mind.*

2 *I've forgotten my PE kit.*
  ▶ to **leave behind** *I've left my PE kit behind.*
    to **not bring** *I haven't brought my PE kit.*
  ← → An opposite is **remember**.

forgive *verb*

I'm sorry. Please forgive my terrible behaviour.
  ▶ to **excuse** to **pardon**

form *noun*

1 *The bicycle is a form of transport.*
  ▶ a **type** a **sort** a **kind**
2 *He is a magician who can change himself into any form he chooses.*
  ▶ a **shape**

form *verb*

These rocks formed millions of years ago.
  ▶ to **develop** to **be made** *These rocks were made millions of years ago.*

foul *adjective*

There was a foul smell in the kitchen.
  ▶ **horrible disgusting nasty revolting repulsive**

a
b
c
d
e
f
g
h
i
j
k
l
m
n
o
p
q
r
s
t
u
v
w
x
y
z

fragile *adjective*
Be careful, these glasses are fragile.
▶ delicate   flimsy   breakable   not very strong
← → An opposite is **strong**.

free *adjective*
1 *At last he was free!*
▶ at liberty   out of prison   no longer in captivity
2 *All the drinks are free.*
▶ for nothing   at no cost

> **"** OTHER WAYS OF SAYING *The drinks are free.*
> *You don't have to pay for them.*
> *There is no charge for them.*

3 *We were given two free tickets for the concert.*
▶ complimentary

free *verb*
The judge freed him.
▶ to release   to liberate
to set free *The judge set him free.*

fresh *adjective*
1 *She changed into some fresh clothes.*
▶ clean   new
2 *Start each answer on a fresh page.*
▶ new   different   clean
3 *I love the taste of fresh strawberries.*
▶ freshly picked
4 *We had fresh bread for tea.*
▶ warm   freshly baked
5 *The fresh air at the seaside will do you good.*
▶ clean   clear   pure
6 *I felt lovely and fresh after my swim.*
▶ lively   energetic   refreshed   invigorated

friend noun
▶ a school friend
a partner (*someone you do a job with*)
a colleague (*someone you work in an office with*)
an ally (*a friend who helps you in a fight*)
a mate (*informal*)
a pal (*informal*)

friendly adjective
1 *She's a very friendly person.*
▶ kind nice pleasant amiable sociable
2 *Don't worry, our dog is very friendly.*
▶ good-natured gentle
3 *I used to dislike her but we're quite friendly now.*
▶ pally (*informal*) matey close
← → An opposite is **unfriendly**.

frighten verb
1 *The sudden noise frightened us.*
▶ to startle to scare
to make someone jump *The noise made me jump.*
to give someone a fright *The noise gave me a fright.*
2 *Stories about monsters used to frighten me when I was young.*
▶ to scare to terrify

frightened adjective
Are you frightened of spiders?
▶ afraid scared terrified (*very frightened*)
petrified (*very frightened indeed*)

frightening adjective
The film was very frightening.
▶ terrifying scary

front noun
At last we got to the front of the queue.
▶ the beginning the head
← → An opposite is **back**.

fruit

fruit *noun*

full *adjective*

1 *We poured water into the bucket until it was full.*
> **full to the brim   overflowing**

2 *The school hall was full.*
> **packed   full to capacity**

3 *The room was full of people.*
> **crowded** *The room was very crowded.*
> **packed** *The room was packed with people.*

4 *The basket was full of good things to eat.*
> **packed with   crammed with   bursting with bulging with**

← → An opposite is **empty**.

fun *noun*

We had lots of fun on the beach.
> **enjoyment   pleasure**

" " OTHER WAYS OF SAYING *We had fun.*
  We enjoyed ourselves.
  We had a good time.

funny *adjective*

1 *He told us a very funny joke.*
> **amusing   hilarious** (*very funny*)   **witty** (*funny and clever*)
← → An opposite is **serious**.

▶▶

2 *We had to write a funny poem.*
▶ humorous
3 *You look really funny in that hat.*
▶ comical   ridiculous
4 *This sauce tastes very funny.*
▶ strange   peculiar   odd   curious

furious *adjective*
My dad was furious when he saw the mess.
▶ livid   fuming

furry *adjective*
I stroked the cat's furry head.
▶ fluffy   woolly   soft

fuss *noun*
1 *There was a terrible fuss when we found a mouse in our classroom.*
▶ a commotion   an uproar
2 *He made a terrible fuss about having his hair cut.*

> ❝❞ OTHER WAYS OF SAYING *He made a fuss.*
> *He complained.*
> *He moaned.*
> *He whinged.*
> *He grumbled.*

fussy *adjective*
1 *Some children are quite fussy about their food.*
▶ choosy   picky   hard to please
2 *My sister is very fussy about keeping her room neat and tidy.*
▶ particular   fastidious

a b c d e **f** g h i j k l m n o p q r s t u v w x y z

Gg

game *noun*
The children were playing a game of football.
▶ a match   a tournament   a competition   a contest

gang *noun*
Do you want to join our gang?
▶ a group   a crowd   a band

gap *noun*
We climbed through a gap in the hedge.
▶ a hole   an opening   a space

gather *verb*
1 People gathered round to watch the jugglers.
▶ to crowd round   to come together   to assemble
2 We gathered blackberries for tea.
▶ to pick   to collect
3 We gathered our things together and left.
▶ to collect   to pick up   to get together
4 I need to gather some information for my project.
▶ to collect   to find

general *adjective*
The general opinion in our class is that school is fun.
▶ common   popular   widespread

generous *adjective*
My grandma is a very generous person.
▶ kind   unselfish   big-hearted
←→ An opposite is **selfish**.

gentle *adjective*

1 *Be gentle with the kitten.*
▶ kind   loving   tender
2 *She's a very gentle child.*
▶ kind   quiet   good-tempered   sweet-tempered
3 *I gave her a gentle tap on the shoulder.*
▶ light   soft
◄ ➔ An opposite is **rough**.

gently *adverb*

He stroked the puppy gently.
▶ softly   lightly   carefully
◄ ➔ An opposite is **roughly**.

get *verb*

1 *I got a new bike for my birthday.*
▶ to receive   to be given
2 *Where can I get some paper?*
▶ to find   to obtain
3 *We're going to the shop to get some food.*
▶ to buy   to purchase
4 *How much money do you get for doing the paper round?*
▶ to earn   to receive
5 *I wonder who will get the first prize.*
▶ to win
6 *Our team got fifteen points.*
▶ to score
7 *I'll go and get the drinks.*
▶ to fetch   to bring
8 *I got chickenpox last winter.*
▶ to catch
9 *What time will we get home?*
▶ to arrive   to reach
10 *I'm getting hungry.*
▶ to become   to grow

ghost *noun*

Have you ever seen a ghost?
▶ a phantom   an apparition   a spirit

a
b
c
d
e
f
g
h
i
j
k
l
m
n
o
p
q
r
s
t
u
v
w
x
y
z

giant *noun*
A wicked giant lived in the castle.
▶ an ogre

giggle *verb*
The girls were all giggling.
▶ to snigger to titter to chuckle

girl *noun*
▶ a lass a kid a child a youngster a teenager

give *verb*
1 I'm going to give Rebecca a CD for her birthday.
▶ to buy
2 My brother gave me his old bike.
▶ to let someone have *My brother let me have his old bike.*
3 I asked for a sweet and she gave me one.
▶ to hand to pass
4 The judges gave the first prize to our team.
▶ to award to present
5 We gave our old toys to the children's hospital.
▶ to donate

glad *adjective*
I'm glad you got here safely.
▶ pleased relieved happy delighted (*very glad*)

glass *noun*
She poured some milk into a glass.
▶ a tumbler a wine glass a beaker a cup

glasses *noun*
I can't see very well without my glasses.
▶ spectacles

glue *noun*
Stick the pieces of paper together with glue.
▶ adhesive gum paste

go *verb*

!!! **go** *is a word that is often overused.*

1 *Let's go along this path.*
▶ **to walk   to run   to continue**

2 *We went slowly along the path.*
▶ **to saunter   to stroll**

3 *She went quickly out of the room.*
▶ **to walk   to march   to stride   to hurry   to rush
to run   to race**

4 *He went downstairs very quietly.*
▶ **to walk   to creep   to sneak   to tiptoe**

5 *My knee was hurting, so I went slowly back to bed.*
▶ **to limp   to hobble   to stagger   to stumble**

6 *The van went slowly forwards.*
▶ **to move**

7 *We went along the motorway for a few miles.*
▶ **to drive   to travel   to speed**

8 *I go to school on my bike.*
▶ **to travel**

9 *We're going at six o'clock.*
▶ **to leave   to set out**

10 *This road goes to London.*
▶ **to lead**

11 *When we got back, our suitcases had gone.*
▶ **to disappear   to vanish**

12 *My watch doesn't go.*
▶ **to work**

13 *When the teacher talks, all of the children go quiet.*
▶ **to become   to grow**

go away *verb*
He told me to go away.
▶ **to leave   to get lost** (*informal*)

go back *verb*
I think we should go back now.
▶ **to return**

go down *verb*
Go down the stairs.
▶ **to descend**

a
b
c
d
e
f
g
h
i
j
k
l
m
n
o
p
q
r
s
t
u
v
w
x
y
z

go into *verb*

Go into the kitchen.
▶ to enter

go out of *verb*

Go out of the house.
▶ to leave   to exit

go up *verb*

Go up the stairs.
▶ to climb   to ascend

good *adjective*

!!! **good** *is a word that is often overused.*

1 *This is a really good book.*
▶ **wonderful brilliant excellent exciting interesting amusing entertaining**

2 *This is very good work.*
▶ **excellent thorough careful**

3 *The children have produced some very good paintings.*
▶ **excellent wonderful brilliant impressive**

4 *William is a very good footballer.*
▶ **skilful talented competent**

5 *I hope the weather is good for sports day.*
▶ **fine nice dry sunny warm**

6 *Have you had a good day at school?*
▶ **nice pleasant enjoyable**

7 *Jessica has got a very good imagination.*
▶ **lively vivid**

8 *He gave the police a good description of the thief.*
▶ **clear vivid precise**

9 *You have been a very good friend to me.*
▶ **kind caring loving loyal**

10 *The children have been very good all day.*
▶ **well-behaved polite**

← → An opposite is **bad**.

grab *verb*

1 *I grabbed my coat and ran out.*
 ▶ to seize   to snatch   to pick up
2 *Tom grabbed my arm.*
 ▶ to take hold of   to grasp   to clutch   to grip

graceful *adjective*

She is a very graceful dancer.
 ▶ elegant   beautiful
 ← → An opposite is **clumsy**.

gradually *adverb*

It gradually got darker.
 ▶ slowly   steadily   progressively   little by little
 ← → An opposite is **suddenly**.

grateful *adjective*

We are very grateful for all your help.
 ▶ thankful
   appreciative *We are very appreciative of all your help.*
 ← → An opposite is **ungrateful**.

great *adjective*

1 *The soldiers led us into a great hall.*
 ▶ big   large   enormous   huge
 ← → An opposite is **small**.
2 *The royal wedding was a great occasion.*
 ▶ grand   magnificent   splendid
 ← → An opposite is **unimportant**.
3 *He was a great musician.*
 ▶ famous   well-known
 ← → An opposite is **terrible**.
4 *It's a great film!*
 ▶ wonderful   brilliant   excellent   fantastic
 ← → An opposite is **terrible**.

green *adjective*

She was wearing a green dress.
 ▶ emerald
   lime green (*bright green*)
   bottle green (*dark green*)

greet verb
She went to the door to greet her guests.
▶ to welcome

grey adjective
1 The sky was grey.
▶ cloudy dull overcast grim forbidding
2 They met an old man with grey hair.
▶ white silver

grin verb
The boy grinned at me.
▶ to smile to beam

grip verb
The old lady gripped my arm.
▶ to hold on to to grasp to clutch

groan verb
We all groaned when the teacher told us we had to stay inside.
▶ to moan to sigh to protest

ground noun
1 Don't leave your bags on the wet ground.
▶ soil earth
2 Who owns this piece of ground?
▶ land territory

group noun
1 There was a large group of people waiting outside the cinema.
▶ a crowd a throng a mob (a large, noisy group)
2 He was showing a group of tourists round the museum.
▶ a party
3 We met up with a group of our friends.
▶ a bunch a crowd a gang (informal)
4 What's your favourite pop group?
▶ a band

••• COLLECTIVE NOUNS FOR SOME GROUPS OF ANIMALS

a flock of birds	a gaggle of geese	a herd of cattle
a flock of sheep	a pack of wolves	a pride of lions
a shoal of fish	a school of whales	

---

group *verb*
We had to group the poems together according to their author.
▶ **to arrange   to classify   to sort   to order**

grow *verb*
1 *Anita has really grown this year.*
▶ **to get bigger   to get taller   to shoot up**
2 *The seeds are starting to grow.*
▶ **to sprout   to shoot up**
3 *The number of children in our school is growing.*
▶ **to increase**
4 *We grow vegetables in our garden.*
▶ **to plant   to produce**

grown-up *noun*
Ask a grown-up if you need help.
▶ **an adult**

grown-up *adjective*
You need to behave in a grown-up manner.
▶ **mature   responsible   sensible**

grumble *verb*
Stop grumbling!
▶ **to complain   to moan   to whinge   to whine**

grumpy *adjective*
Why are you so grumpy today?
▶ **cross   bad-tempered   sulky   moody**
← → An opposite is **good-tempered**.

guard *verb*
1 *Soldiers guard the castle.*
▶ **to protect   to defend**
2 *Who will guard the prisoner?*
▶ **to watch   to keep an eye on**
3 *A mother elephant will guard her young.*
▶ **to look after   to watch over   to protect**

a
b
c
d
e
f
g
h
i
j
k
l
m
n
o
p
q
r
s
t
u
v
w
x
y
z

a
b
c
d
e
f
g
h
i
j
k
l
m
n
o
p
q
r
s
t
u
v
w
x
y
z

guard *noun*
There was a guard by the door.
▶ a sentry   a lookout
a security officer (*in a bank, office, or shop*)

guess *verb*
1 *Can you guess how many sweets are in the jar?*
▶ to estimate
2 *Because they were late, I guessed that their car must have broken down.*
▶ to think   to suppose   to predict   to infer

guilty *adjective*
1 *The jury decided that he was guilty.*
←→ An opposite is **innocent**.

> 6 9 OTHER WAYS OF SAYING *He was guilty.*
> *He had committed the crime.*
> *He was the culprit.*

2 *I felt guilty because I had been mean to my sister.*
▶ bad   ashamed   remorseful

gun *noun*
The man was holding a gun in his hand.
▶ a weapon   a firearm

> ••• SOME TYPES OF GUN
> a machine gun   an air pistol   a pistol
> a revolver   a rifle   a shotgun

hair *noun*

 Focus on **hair**

She had blonde hair.
- ▶ **locks** (*long hair*)
  curls (*curly hair*)

SOME WORDS YOU MIGHT USE TO DESCRIBE THE COLOUR OF
SOMEONE'S HAIR

auburn	black	blond	brown
chestnut	dark	jet black	fair
ginger	grey	mousy	red
sandy	white		

SOME WORDS YOU MIGHT USE TO DESCRIBE SOMEONE'S HAIR

curly	beautiful	dishevelled	fine
frizzy	glossy	long	straight
sleek	scruffy	shiny	short
thick	tousled	untidy	wavy
windswept			

hairy *adjective*
They were greeted by a large, hairy dog.
- ▶ **furry   shaggy   woolly**

handsome *adjective*
He is a very handsome man.
- ▶ **good-looking   attractive   gorgeous**
- ← → An opposite is **ugly**.

hang *verb*
1 *A bunch of keys was hanging from his belt.*
- ▶ **to dangle**

2 *He hung on to the rope.*
- ▶ **to hold on to   to cling on to**

a
b
c
d
e
f
g
h
i
j
k
l
m
n
o
p
q
r
s
t
u
v
w
x
y
z

happen *verb*
When did the accident happen?
▶ to take place   to occur

happy *adjective*
1 *I'm feeling very happy today.*
▶ cheerful   in a good mood
2 *We were happy when we won the cup.*
▶ pleased   delighted   thrilled   overjoyed
3 *She's a happy child.*
▶ cheerful   contented   good-humoured
←→ An opposite is **unhappy**.

hard *adjective*
1 *The ground was hard and frozen.*
▶ firm   solid
←→ An opposite is **soft**.
2 *The frame is made of hard plastic.*
▶ stiff   rigid
←→ An opposite is **soft**.
3 *The teacher gave us some very hard sums to do.*
▶ difficult   complicated   tricky   challenging
←→ An opposite is **easy**.
4 *Carrying the bricks was very hard work.*
▶ tiring   exhausting   strenuous   back-breaking
←→ An opposite is **easy**.

hardly *adverb*
I was so tired I could hardly walk.
▶ scarcely   barely   only just

harm *verb*
1 *I didn't mean to harm you.*
▶ to hurt   to injure
2 *Smoking can harm your health.*
▶ to damage   to ruin

harmful *adjective*

1 *Smoking is harmful to your health.*
- ▶ **bad for** *Smoking is bad for your health.*
  damaging *Smoking is damaging to your health.*

2 *Be careful of these harmful chemicals.*
- ▶ **dangerous   poisonous   toxic**

← → An opposite is **harmless**.

harmless *adjective*

Our dog seems fierce, but really he is harmless.
- ▶ **safe**

← → An opposite is **dangerous**.

> " OTHER WAYS OF SAYING *He is harmless.*
> *He won't harm you.*
> *He won't hurt you.*
> *He's not dangerous.*
> *He's very gentle.*

harsh *adjective*

1 *The machine made a harsh sound.*
- ▶ **rough   shrill   grating**

← → An opposite is **gentle**.

2 *She spoke in a harsh voice.*
- ▶ **shrill   piercing**

← → An opposite is **gentle**.

3 *That punishment seemed a bit harsh.*
- ▶ **hard   severe   strict   unkind**

← → An opposite is **lenient**.

hat *noun*

••• SOME TYPES OF HAT

a baseball cap	a beret	a boater
a bonnet	a bowler hat	a cap
a fedora	a fez	a helmet
a panama	a sombrero	a top hat
a turban	a woolly hat	

hate *verb*
I hate cold weather!
  ▶ to detest   to dislike   to loathe
    to not be able to stand *I can't stand cold weather!*
    to not be able to bear *I can't bear cold weather!*
  ←▶ An opposite is **love**.

have *verb*
1 *Our school has fifteen computers.*
  ▶ to own   to possess
2 *I had some lovely presents for my birthday.*
  ▶ to get   to receive
3 *My brother is at home because he has chickenpox.*
  ▶ to be suffering from *He is suffering from chickenpox.*
    to be infected with *He is infected with chickenpox.*

heal *verb*
That cut on your arm will soon heal.
  ▶ to get better   to mend

healthy *adjective*
1 *Most of the children here are very healthy.*
  ▶ strong   well   fit
2 *This food is very healthy.*
  ▶ nutritious   nourishing   good for you
  ←▶ An opposite is **unhealthy**.

heap *noun*
There was a heap of dirty clothes on the floor.
  ▶ a pile   a mound   a mass   a stack

hear *verb*
1 *I can't hear what he's saying.*
  ▶ to make out
2 *I'm sorry, I didn't quite hear that.*
  ▶ to catch
3 *Did you hear the weather forecast on the radio?*
  ▶ to listen to

heat *noun*
I could feel the heat from the fire.
  ▶ warmth

heat *verb*
We can heat up some soup for lunch.
▶ to warm up

heavy *adjective*
This bag is very heavy.
▶ not light   weighty
← → An opposite is **light**.

> **6 9**   ANOTHER WAY OF SAYING *This bag is heavy.*
> *This bag weighs a lot.*

help *verb*
1 *Shall I help you with your bags?*
▶ to assist
to give someone a hand *Shall I give you a hand?*
2 *Didn't anybody help you?*
▶ to assist   to take pity on   to come to someone's aid
3 *Members of a team must all help each other.*
▶ to support   to cooperate with

help *noun*
Do you need some help?
▶ assistance   advice   support

helpful *adjective*
She is always very helpful in class.
▶ kind   considerate   willing
← → An opposite is **unhelpful**.

helping *noun*
He gave me a huge helping of chips.
▶ a portion   a serving

here *adjective*
Are all the children here?
▶ present

hesitate *verb*
She hesitated before diving into the water.
▶ to pause   to wait

a
b
c
d
e
f
g
h
i
j
k
l
m
n
o
p
q
r
s
t
u
v
w
x
y
z

hide *verb*

1 *We hid in the garden shed.*
▶ to keep out of sight

2 *The thieves decided to hide for a while.*
▶ to go into hiding to lie low

3 *They hid the money in a hollow tree.*
▶ to conceal to stash

high *adjective*

1 *There are a lot of high buildings in the city.*
▶ tall big towering

2 *Some shops charge very high prices.*
▶ inflated exorbitant

3 *She spoke in a high voice.*
▶ high-pitched piercing shrill squeaky
←→ An opposite is **low**.

hill *noun*

We walked up the hill.
▶ a mountain a slope

hit *verb*

1 *You shouldn't hit your little brother.*
▶ to punch to thump to slap to strike to smack

2 *His master used to hit him with a stick.*
▶ to beat to thrash to whip

3 *I fell and hit my elbow.*
▶ to knock to bang to bash to bump

4 *The car went out of control and hit a lamppost.*
▶ to bump into to crash into to smash into to collide with
to ram (*to hit deliberately*) *Another car rammed our car from behind.*

5 *He ran into the road and a car hit him.*
▶ to run over *A car ran him over.*
to knock down *A car knocked him down.*

hoarse *adjective*

Dad's voice was hoarse because he had a cold.
▶ croaking deep husky rough

hobby *noun*
Skateboarding is my favourite hobby.
▶ a pastime   an interest   an activity   a leisure activity

hold *verb*
1 Can I hold the puppy?
▶ to carry   to cuddle
2 Hold the handrail as you go up the steps.
▶ to grip   to grasp
3 He was holding a torch.
▶ to carry
to have in your hand He had a torch in his hand.
4 One of the men was holding a knife.
▶ to brandish   to wield
5 This box holds twenty pencils.
▶ to take   to contain
to have space for This box has space for twenty pencils.

hole *noun*
1 We climbed through a hole in the hedge.
▶ an opening   a gap   a space
2 There was a big hole in the ground.
▶ a pit   a crater   a chasm (a very big, deep hole)
3 The tiny animal escaped back into its hole.
▶ a burrow   a den   a nest
4 I could see them through a hole in the wall.
▶ a crack   a slit   a chink
5 There's a hole in my shirt.
▶ a split   a rip   a tear
6 There was a hole in one of the water pipes.
▶ a crack   a leak
7 One of my bicycle tyres has a hole in it.
▶ a puncture

holy *adjective*
He read to us from the holy book.
▶ sacred   religious

a b c d e f g h i j k l m n o p q r s t u v w x y z

home *noun*

  1 *This is my home.*
    ▶ a residence a house a flat an apartment

> **❝ ❞** OTHER WAYS OF SAYING *This is my home.*
>   *This is where I live.*
>   *This is the place where I live.*

  2 *He is very poor and has no home.*
    ▶ a place to live *He has no place to live.*

honest *adjective*

  1 *I'm sure he is an honest man.*
    ▶ good trustworthy law-abiding
    ←→ An opposite is **dishonest**.
  2 *Did you enjoy the film? Be honest.*
    ▶ truthful sincere frank
    ←→ An opposite is **insincere**.

hopeless *adjective*

  I'm hopeless at swimming.
    ▶ bad no good terrible useless
  ←→ An opposite is **good**.

horrible *adjective*

  1 *Don't be horrible!*
    ▶ nasty unpleasant mean unkind obnoxious horrid
  2 *The food was horrible.*
    ▶ revolting disgusting tasteless inedible
  3 *What a horrible colour!*
    ▶ revolting vile hideous repulsive
  4 *The weather was horrible.*
    ▶ awful dreadful terrible appalling
  5 *I had a dream about a horrible monster.*
    ▶ terrible frightening terrifying
  ←→ An opposite is **pleasant**.

horrid *adjective*
Everyone is being horrid to me!
▶ **nasty unkind mean horrible**
◀ ▶ An opposite is **pleasant**.

horror *noun*
The sight of the huge beast filled me with horror.
▶ **fear terror dread**

horse *noun*
▶ a **pony**
a **nag** (*an old horse*)
a **steed** (*a big, strong horse*)
a **mare** (*a female horse*)
a **stallion** (*a male horse*)
a **foal** (*a baby horse*)
a **colt** (*a young horse*)

Focus on **horse**

SOME TYPES OF HORSE
a **carthorse**   a **racehorse**   a **Shetland pony**
a **Shire horse**

SOME WORDS YOU MIGHT USE TO DESCRIBE THE COLOUR OF A
HORSE
black
bay (*reddish brown*)
chestnut
dapple-grey
roan (*brown or black, with some white hairs*)
piebald (*with patches of different colours*)
skewbald (*with patches of white and another colour*)
white

SOME WORDS YOU MIGHT USE TO DESCRIBE HOW A HORSE
WALKS OR RUNS
to trot   **to canter**   **to gallop**

---

a
b
c
d
e
f
g
h
i
j
k
l
m
n
o
p
q
r
s
t
u
v
w
x
y
z

hot *adjective*

1 *It was a lovely hot day.*
> **warm   boiling hot   baking hot   scorching hot   sweltering** (*too hot*)

← → An opposite is **cold**.

2 *Be careful with that pan—it's hot.*
> **red hot   burning hot**

← → An opposite is **cold**.

3 *We sat down in front of the hot fire.*
> **warm   blazing   roaring**

← → An opposite is **cold**.

4 *He spilled hot water over himself.*
> **boiling   scalding   scalding hot**

← → An opposite is **cold**.

5 *They brought us bowls of hot soup.*
> **warm   piping hot** (*very hot*)

← → An opposite is **cold**.

6 *We add spices to food to make it hot.*
> **spicy**

← → An opposite is **mild**.

house *noun*
> **a home**

• • •   SOME TYPES OF HOUSE
a bungalow   a cottage   a mansion   a palace

hug *verb*
He hugged his mother.
> **to cuddle   to hold   to embrace**

huge *adjective*
The huge creature came after them.
> **great   enormous   gigantic   massive**

← → An opposite is **tiny**.

hungry *adjective*
1 *I'm glad it's lunchtime, I'm hungry.*
  ▶ **starving   famished**
  ravenous (*very hungry*)
  peckish (*slightly hungry*)
2 *The people have no food, and their children are hungry.*
  ▶ **starving   underfed   undernourished**

hunt *verb*
1 *Lions hunt deer and other animals.*
  ▶ **to chase   to kill**
2 *Will you help me hunt for my purse?*
  ▶ **to look for   to search for**

hurry *verb*
1 *Come on, hurry up!*
  ▶ **to be quick** *Come on, be quick!*
  to get a move on (*informal*)   *Come on, get a move on!*
2 *He hurried out of the room.*
  ▶ **to rush   to dash   to run   to race**

hurt *verb*
1 *You mustn't hurt animals.*
  ▶ **to injure   to harm**
2 *My head is hurting.*
  ▶ **to ache   to throb   to pound**
3 *The cut on my leg still hurts.*
  ▶ **to be sore   to be painful   to sting   to smart**
4 *I fell and hurt my leg.*
  ▶ **to injure   to cut   to graze   to bruise   to sprain   to twist
  to dislocate   to break**

hut *noun*
We slept in a little hut in the wood.
  ▶ **a shack   a cabin   a shelter   a shed**

a b c d e f g h i j k l m n o p q r s t u v w x y z

Ii

idea noun
1 *I've got an idea!*
▶ **a suggestion   a plan   a thought   a brainwave**
2 *The teacher gave us some useful ideas about how to do well in the test.*
▶ **a suggestion   a tip   a piece of advice**
3 *I don't always agree with your ideas.*
▶ **an opinion   a belief**
4 *The film gave us an idea of what life was like in ancient Rome.*
▶ **an impression   a picture**

ideal adjective
The weather was ideal for a picnic.
▶ **perfect   excellent   just right**

ignore verb
I said hello to them, but they ignored me.
▶ **to take no notice of** *They took no notice of me.*
to pay no attention to *They paid no attention to me.*

ill adjective
I felt too ill to go to school.
▶ **unwell   poorly   sick**
← → An opposite is **healthy**.

illness noun
She has now recovered from her illness.
▶ **a disease** (*a serious illness*)
an infection (*one you catch from other people*)
a bug (*one that is not very serious*)

imaginary *adjective*

1 *Dragons are imaginary animals.*
▶ **mythical fictional legendary**
2 *She has an imaginary friend.*
▶ **invented made-up**
3 *We played on an imaginary boat.*
▶ **pretend**
◆➔ An opposite is **real**.

imagine *verb*

1 *I tried to imagine what life was like in Roman times.*
▶ **to think about to picture to visualize to envisage**
2 *It didn't really happen. You only imagined it.*
▶ **to dream**

immediately *adverb*

Come here immediately!
▶ **at once straightaway this minute instantly**

important *adjective*

1 *There is one important thing you must remember.*
▶ **vital crucial essential**
2 *I've got an important message for you.*
▶ **urgent**
3 *The World Cup is an important sporting event.*
▶ **big major significant**
4 *Today is a very important day.*
▶ **special significant**
5 *I was nervous about meeting such an important person.*
▶ **famous distinguished prominent**
◆➔ An opposite is **unimportant**.

impossible *adjective*

I can't do that—it's impossible!
▶ **not possible not humanly possible not feasible**
◆➔ An opposite is **possible**.

improve *verb*

1 *Your maths is improving.*
▶ **to get better to come on**
2 *Try to improve your handwriting.*
▶ **to make progress with**

increase *verb*

1 *Our class has increased in size.*
▶ to get bigger   to grow   to expand
2 *The noise gradually increased.*
▶ to get louder   to build up
3 *The price of tickets has increased.*
▶ to go up   to rise
to double (*to become twice as much*)
←→ An opposite is **decrease**.

incredible *adjective*

1 *It seems incredible that someone could survive for so long in the desert.*
▶ **unbelievable   extraordinary   unlikely unimaginable**
2 *It's an incredible film!*
▶ **great   excellent   brilliant   wonderful   fantastic amazing**

information *noun*

1 *We are collecting information about rainforests.*
▶ **facts   details**
2 *All the information is stored on the computer.*
▶ **data**

injection *noun*

The doctor gave me an injection.
▶ **a jab**

injure *verb*

1 *He fell and injured his leg.*
▶ to hurt   to cut   to graze   to bruise
2 *I landed on my wrist and injured it.*
▶ to sprain   to twist   to dislocate   to break

injury *noun*

The captain couldn't play because he had an injury.
▶ a wound   a cut   a bruise   a burn
a graze (*a small cut*)
a gash (*a big cut*)

innocent *adjective*
The jury decided that he was innocent.
  ▶ not guilty blameless
←→ An opposite is **guilty**.

insect *noun*

 Focus on **insect**

  ▶ a bug a creepy-crawly

SOME TYPES OF INSECT

an ant	a bee	a beetle
a bluebottle	a bumble bee	a butterfly
a cricket	a daddy-long-legs	a dragonfly
a fly	a grasshopper	a ladybird
a locust	a midge	a mosquito
a moth	a stick insect	a wasp
	a woodlouse	

SOME WORDS YOU MIGHT USE TO DESCRIBE HOW AN INSECT FLIES
to fly   to buzz
to swarm (*to fly in large numbers*)

SOME WORDS YOU MIGHT USE TO DESCRIBE HOW AN INSECT MOVES
to crawl   to scuttle   to scurry

inspect *verb*
He inspected the cup to see if it was cracked.
  ▶ to examine to check to look at

instant *adjective*
The film was an instant success.
  ▶ immediate instantaneous

instruct *verb*
1 *The judo teacher instructs us on move safety.*
  ▶ to coach to teach to train
2 *The fire chief instructed everyone to leave the building.*
  ▶ to order to command to tell

a
b
c
d
e
f
g
h
i
j
k
l
m
n
o
p
q
r
s
t
u
v
w
x
y
z

a
b
c
d
e
f
g
h
i
j
k
l
m
n
o
p
q
r
s
t
u
v
w
x
y
z

instructions *noun*
Read the instructions on the packet carefully.
▶ **directions guidelines**

insult *verb*
She insulted me by saying I was stupid.
▶ **to abuse**

> ❝ ❞ OTHER WAYS OF SAYING *She insulted me.*
> *She was rude to me.*
> *She called me names.*

intelligent *adjective*
He's a very intelligent boy.
▶ **clever bright brainy quick sharp smart**
←▶ An opposite is **stupid**.

intend *verb*
1 *I didn't intend to upset her.*
▶ **to mean to want to plan**
2 *We intend to set up a school football team next year.*
▶ **to plan to propose to aim**

interested *adjective*
I'm very interested in old coins.
▶ **fascinated** *I'm fascinated by old coins.*

interesting *adjective*
We found some interesting old documents.
▶ **fascinating intriguing**
←▶ An opposite is **boring**.

interfere *verb*
She's always interfering!
▶ **to meddle to stick your nose in** *She's always sticking her nose in!*

interrupt *verb*
Please don't interrupt when I'm talking.
▶ **to butt in to barge in**

interval *noun*
You can have an ice cream during the interval.
► a break   an interlude   an intermission

invade *verb*
The Romans invaded Britain.
► to attack   to occupy   to march into

invent *verb*
Who invented the first computer?
► to design   to develop   to create   to make

investigate *verb*
We had to investigate how the Romans lived for our homework.
► to explore   to look into   to research   to study

invisible *adjective*
Ivy had grown over the old door and made it invisible.
► hidden   concealed
← → An opposite is **visible**.

invite *verb*
I've invited all my friends to the party.
► to ask

irritate *verb*
My little brother keeps irritating me!
► to annoy   to pester   to bother
to get on someone's nerves *My little brother is getting on my nerves.*

irritated *adjective*
I was beginning to feel irritated.
► cross   annoyed   angry   exasperated

irritating *adjective*
He has some very irritating habits.
► annoying   infuriating   maddening

a b c d e f g h i j k l m n o p q r s t u v w x y z

Jj

jab *noun*
The doctor gave me a jab.
► an injection

jail *noun*
He was locked up in jail.
► prison   a cell   a dungeon

jam *verb*
The door jammed and we couldn't open it.
► to stick   to get stuck

jar *noun*
We bought a jar of honey.
► a pot

jealous *adjective*
I felt a little bit jealous when I saw her new bike.
► envious   resentful

jet *noun*
A jet of water spurted out of the pipe.
► a stream   a spray   a fountain

jewel *noun*
We found a box full of diamonds and other jewels.
► a gem   a precious stone

••• SOME TYPES OF JEWEL

a diamond	an emerald	a pearl
a ruby	a sapphire	an opal
jet		

SOME TYPES OF JEWELLERY

a bracelet	a brooch	a crown
earrings	a necklace	a ring
a tiara		

job *noun*

1 *I want to have an interesting job.*
▶ an occupation   a profession   work   a career

2 *I had to do a couple of jobs for my mum.*
▶ a chore   a task

join *verb*

1 *Join the two wires together.*
▶ to fix   to fasten   to attach   to connect   to tie   to stick
   to glue

2 *Why don't you join your local drama group?*
▶ to become a member of

joke *noun*

1 *He told us some funny jokes.*
▶ a funny story   a gag

2 *She hid my school bag as a joke.*
▶ a trick   a prank

journey *noun*

He set out on his long journey.
▶ a trip   an expedition
   a voyage (*a journey by sea*)
   a flight (*a journey in a plane*)
   a drive (*a journey by car*)
   a trek (*a long journey on foot*)

jumble *noun*

1 *There was a jumble of books on her desk.*
▶ a pile   a heap   a mass

2 *Everything was in a complete jumble.*
▶ a mess   a muddle

jump *verb*

1 *He jumped and caught the ball.*
▶ to leap   to spring

2 *The cat jumped on the mouse.*
▶ to leap   to pounce   to spring

3 *She was jumping for joy.*
▶ to leap about   to prance about   to skip about

▶▶

jungle

4 *He jumped over the fence.*
> ▶ **to leap over   to vault over
> to hurdle** *He hurdled the fence.*
> **to clear** *He cleared the fence.*

5 *She jumped into the water.*
> ▶ **to leap   to dive   to plunge**

6 *The sudden noise made me jump.*
> ▶ **to start   to flinch**

jungle *noun*
These animals live deep in the jungle.
> ▶ **a forest   a tropical forest   a rainforest**

junk *noun*
The garage was full of old junk.
> ▶ **rubbish   odds and ends**

just *adverb*
1 *This is just what I wanted.*
> ▶ **exactly   precisely**

2 *The classroom is just big enough for all the children.*
> ▶ **only just   hardly   barely   scarcely**

3 *She has just left.*
> ▶ **only just   only recently**

keen *adjective*

1 *Most boys are keen on football.*
▶ **enthusiastic about   fond of**

2 *She was keen to go with her sisters.*
▶ **eager**

keep *verb*

1 *He found some money and kept it.*
▶ **to hold on to** *He held on to the money.*
to keep possession of *He kept possession of the money.*

2 *Keep still!*
▶ **to stay   to remain**

3 *They keep chickens on their farm.*
▶ **to have   to look after**

4 *I told him to be quiet, but he kept talking.*
▶ **to continue   to carry on**

kill *verb*

1 *Someone has killed the president.*
▶ **to murder   to assassinate**
to take someone's life *They took the president's life.*

2 *In the past, people used to kill criminals instead of sending them to prison.*
▶ **to execute   to put to death** *They used to put criminals to death.*

3 *The soldiers killed hundreds of innocent people.*
▶ **to slaughter   to massacre**

4 *A butcher kills animals and sells their meat.*
▶ **to slaughter**

5 *Sometimes a vet has to kill an animal if it is badly injured.*
▶ **to destroy** *The injured horse had to be destroyed.*
to put down *The vet put the old dog down.*
to put to sleep *The vet put the old dog to sleep.*

a
b
c
d
e
f
g
h
i
j
k
l
m
n
o
p
q
r
s
t
u
v
w
x
y
z

kind *adjective*

1 *It was very kind of you to help us.*
  ▶ **good considerate thoughtful**

2 *He's a very kind boy.*
  ▶ **gentle good-natured kind-hearted thoughtful unselfish**

3 *It was very kind of you to give so much money to the school.*
  ▶ **generous**

← → An opposite is **unkind**.

kind *noun*

1 *A dictionary is a kind of book.*
  ▶ **a type a sort**

2 *A terrier is a kind of dog.*
  ▶ **a breed**

3 *A ladybird is a kind of beetle.*
  ▶ **a species**

4 *What kind of trainers do you want to buy?*
  ▶ **a brand a make**

kneel *verb*

I knelt down beside him.
  ▶ **to bend to stoop to crouch**

knife *noun*

```
• • •   SOME TYPES OF KNIFE
          a carving knife   a dagger   a kitchen knife
          a penknife
```

knob *noun*

1 *He turned the door knob.*
  ▶ **a handle**

2 *She started fiddling with the knobs on the machine.*
  ▶ **a switch a button a control**

knock *verb*

1 *I knocked on the door.*
- ▶ **to rap** **to tap**
  to bang (*to knock loudly*)
  to hammer (*to knock very loudly*)

2 *I fell and knocked my head.*
- ▶ **to bang** **to bump** **to hit** **to bash**

knock over *verb*

Someone's knocked over the bucket of water.
- ▶ **to overturn** **to upset**

know *verb*

1 *Do you know how a car works?*
- ▶ **to understand**

2 *Do you know what day it is?*
- ▶ **to remember**
  to be aware *Are you aware what day it is?*

3 *I knew that someone was watching me.*
- ▶ **to sense**
  to be aware *I was aware that someone was watching me.*

4 *Do you know my sister?*
- ▶ **to be a friend of** *Are you a friend of my sister?*
  to be acquainted with *Are you acquainted with my sister?*

a
b
c
d
e
f
g
h
i
j
k
l
m
n
o
p
q
r
s
t
u
v
w
x
y
z

Ll

land noun

1 This is good land for growing crops.
▶ ground   earth   soil

2 He has travelled to many lands.
▶ a country   a nation
a kingdom (a land with a king or queen)

land verb

1 The plane should land at seven o'clock.
▶ to touch down   to come down   to arrive

2 They rowed towards the island and landed on a small beach.
▶ to come ashore   to go ashore

3 The bird landed on a small branch.
▶ to alight   to fly down onto

large adjective

1 Paris is a large city.
▶ big   huge   enormous
immense (very large)

2 They live in a large house.
▶ big   spacious   roomy   huge   massive
gigantic (very large)

3 She gave me a large portion of chips.
▶ big   generous   sizeable

← → An opposite is small.

last adjective

Z is the last letter of the alphabet.
▶ final

← → An opposite is first.

last verb

The film lasted for two hours.
▶ to continue   to go on

late *adjective*
The bus was late.
> ▸ delayed   overdue
> ←→ An opposite is **early**.

lately *adverb*
Have you seen any good films lately?
> ▸ recently

laugh *verb*
All the children started laughing.
> ▸ to giggle   to chuckle   to titter   to snigger
> to guffaw (*to laugh very loudly*)
> to burst out laughing (*to start laughing*)
> to roar with laughter   to shriek with laughter

laugh at *verb*
All the other children laugh at him.
> ▸ to make fun of   to tease   to mock

law *noun*
Everyone must obey the laws of the country.
> ▸ a rule

lay *verb*
1 *I laid the clothes on my bed.*
> ▸ to put   to place   to spread
2 *Whose turn is it to lay the table for tea?*
> ▸ to set

layer *noun*
1 *There was a thick layer of dust on the old books.*
> ▸ a coating   a covering   a film
2 *The pond was covered in a layer of ice.*
> ▸ a sheet

lazy *adjective*
Get up! Don't be so lazy!
> ▸ idle   indolent

a
b
c
d
e
f
g
h
i
j
k
l
m
n
o
p
q
r
s
t
u
v
w
x
y
z

Lead

Lead *verb*

1 *He led us to the secret cave.*
▶ to take   to guide

2 *Who is going to lead the expedition?*
▶ to command   to be in charge of

3 *Our team was leading at the end of the first round.*
▶ to be winning
to be in the lead *Our team was in the lead.*

Leader *noun*

Who is the leader of your gang?
▶ the boss   the chief   the captain

Leak *verb*

1 *Water was leaking out of the pipe.*
▶ to drip   to trickle   to seep   to spill

2 *My bottle is leaking.*
▶ to have a hole in

Lean *verb*

1 *She leaned forward to look out of the window.*
▶ to stretch   to bend

2 *The old building leans to one side.*
▶ to slant   to tilt

3 *He was leaning against the wall.*
▶ to recline

4 *He leaned his bicycle against the wall.*
▶ to prop   to rest

Leap *verb*

1 *The cat leaped into the air.*
▶ to jump   to spring

2 *She leaped over the fence.*
▶ to jump over   to vault over
to hurdle *She hurdled the fence.*
to clear *She cleared the fence.*

3 *She leaped into the water.*
▶ to jump   to dive   to plunge

Learn *verb*

We are learning about the Vikings at school.
- ▶ to find out   to discover

Leave *verb*

1 *What time does the train leave?*
- ▶ to go   to set off   to depart
- ← → An opposite is **arrive**.

2 *The ship leaves at nine o'clock.*
- ▶ to sail   to depart

3 *The plane leaves at eleven thirty.*
- ▶ to take off   to depart

4 *She left quietly when no one was looking.*
- ▶ to sneak off   to slip away   to creep off

5 *He left in a terrible temper.*
- ▶ to go off   to storm off   to stomp off

6 *Where did you leave your bag?*
- ▶ to put

7 *They left the puppy in the street.*
- ▶ to abandon

8 *All my friends went away and left me!*
- ▶ to desert   to abandon

Lend *verb*

Will you lend me your pen?
- ▶ to loan
- to let someone borrow *Will you let me borrow your pen?*

> 6 9 OTHER WAYS OF SAYING *Will you lend me your pen?*
>   *Can I borrow your pen?*
>   *Can I use your pen?*

Let *verb*

Will you let me ride your bike?
- ▶ to allow *Will you allow me to ride your bike?*
- to give someone permission *Will you give me permission to ride your bike?*

level *adjective*

1 *You need a nice level surface to work on.*
  ▶ flat even smooth horizontal
  ←→ An opposite is **uneven**.
2 *Their scores were level at half time.*
  ▶ even equal the same
  ←→ An opposite is **different**.

lid *noun*

Put the lid back on the jar.
  ▶ a top a cap a cover

lie *noun*

Don't tell lies!
  ▶ a fib an untruth

lie *verb*

1 *She was lying on her bed.*
  ▶ to recline to lounge
  to be stretched out *She was stretched out on her bed.*
  to be sprawled *She was sprawled on her bed.*
2 *I don't believe him—I think he's lying.*
  ▶ to fib to tell lies *I think he's telling lies.*
  to not tell the truth *I think he's not telling the truth.*

lift *noun*

1 *We took the lift up to the fifth floor.*
  ▶ an elevator
2 *He gave us a lift in his new car.*
  ▶ a ride

lift *verb*

1 *She lifted the boy into the air.*
  ▶ to raise to hoist
2 *He lifted one of the books off the shelf.*
  ▶ to pick up

a b c d e f g h i j k l m n o p q r s t u v w x y z

light *adjective*

1 *My suitcase is quite light.*
- ▶ **not very heavy**
- ←→ An opposite is **heavy**.

> ❝ ❞ ANOTHER WAY OF SAYING *My suitcase is light.*
> *My suitcase does not weigh very much.*

2 *Our classroom is nice and light.*
- ▶ **bright well-lit**
- ←→ An opposite is **dim**.

3 *She was wearing light blue trousers.*
- ▶ **pale pastel**
- ←→ An opposite is **dark**.

light *noun*

Focus on **light**

1 *I couldn't see very well because there wasn't much light.*
- ▶ **daylight sunlight moonlight**

2 *I managed to find my way using the light from my torch.*
- ▶ **brightness glow**

3 *Please could you switch the light on?*
- ▶ **an electric light a lamp**

SOME TYPES OF LIGHT
floodlights (*lights at a sports ground*)
a headlight (*a light on a car*)
a searchlight (*a powerful torch*)
a spotlight (*a light on a stage*)
a streetlight

SOME WORDS YOU MIGHT USE TO DESCRIBE HOW LIGHT
SHINES

to shine	to glow	to gleam
to glimmer	to glisten	to glimmer
to sparkle	to sparkle	to twinkle
to flash	to flicker	
to glare (*to shine very brightly*)		

like

like *preposition*
Your pencil case is like mine.
▶ the same as   similar to   identical to

like *verb*
1 *I like our new teacher.*
▶ to get on well with
to be fond of *I am fond of our new teacher.*
to love (*to like a lot*)
to idolize (*to like very much*)
2 *I like ice cream.*
▶ to be keen on *I am keen on ice cream.*
to enjoy   to love
to adore (*to like very much*)
3 *I think that boy likes you!*
▶ to fancy
4 *Would you like a drink?*
←→ An opposite is **dislike**.

> " OTHER WAYS OF SAYING *Would you like a drink?*
> *Do you want a drink?*
> *Do you fancy a drink?*

likely *adjective*
It's quite likely that it will rain later.
▶ possible   probable   to be expected
←→ An opposite is **unlikely**.

limp *verb*
She was limping because her foot hurt.
▶ to hobble

line *noun*
1 *Draw a line across the top of the page.*
▶ a mark
2 *His trousers had a white line down each side.*
▶ a stripe

▶▶

3 *Her old face was covered in lines.*
▶ **wrinkles**
4 *We all stood in a line.*
▶ **a row   a queue**

listen *verb*
Please listen to what I am going to say.
▶ **to pay attention**

litter *noun*
The playground was covered in litter.
▶ **rubbish   mess**

little *adjective*
1 *We've only got a little car.*
▶ **small   tiny   titchy**
2 *They live in a little house on the edge of the village.*
▶ **small   tiny   cramped   poky**
3 *He's only a little boy.*
▶ **young**
4 *It's only a little problem.*
▶ **small   slight   minor**
5 *We had a little chat.*
▶ **short   brief**
← → An opposite is **big**.

live *adjective*
He brought a live snake into school.
▶ **living**

live *verb*
1 *Plants cannot live without water.*
▶ **to exist   to survive   to remain alive**
2 *We live in London.*
▶ **to reside**

a
b
c
d
e
f
g
h
i
j
k
l
m
n
o
p
q
r
s
t
u
v
w
x
y
z

lively *adjective*
The puppies were lively.
▶ active busy energetic boisterous playful
←→ An opposite is **quiet**.

load *verb*
1 *We loaded the suitcases into the car.*
▶ to put to lift
2 *We loaded the trolley with food.*
▶ to fill to pack to pile up

lock *noun*
We need to put a lock on the shed door.
▶ a bolt a padlock

lock *verb*
Don't forget to lock the door.
▶ to shut to fasten to bolt to secure

lonely *adjective*
1 *I felt lonely when all my friends had left.*
▶ alone isolated friendless
2 *They live in a lonely farmhouse.*
▶ remote isolated

long *adjective*
1 *It's quite a long film.*
▶ lengthy
2 *We had to sit and listen to his long speech.*
▶ endless interminable long-drawn-out
←→ An opposite is **short**.

look *verb*

!!! **look** is a word that is often overused.

1 *I'm looking at a squirrel in the garden.*
▶ to watch to observe to study
2 *I looked quickly into the box.*
▶ to glance to peep ▶▶

Look *verb (coninued)*

> **3** *She looked at the picture for a long time.*
>   ▸ **to stare   to gaze**
> **4** *He looked at me angrily.*
>   ▸ **to glare   to glower   to scowl**
> **5** *She looked at the tiny writing, trying to read it.*
>   ▸ **to peer   to squint**
> **6** *That dog doesn't look very friendly.*
>   ▸ **to seem   to appear**

Look after *verb*

I have to look after my little brother.
  ▸ **to take care of   to care for   to mind   to keep an eye on**

Look for *verb*

I'll help you look for your purse.
  ▸ **to search for   to hunt for   to try to find**

Look like *verb*

She looks like her brother.
  ▸ **to be similar to** *She is similar to her brother.*
  to resemble *She resembles her brother.*

Loose *adjective*

1 *One of my teeth is loose.*
  ▸ **wobbly   shaky**
  ←▸ An opposite is **secure**.
2 *The rope was a bit loose.*
  ▸ **slack**
  ←▸ An opposite is **tight**.
3 *I like to wear loose clothes.*
  ▸ **baggy   big   oversized**
  ←▸ An opposite is **tight**.
4 *One of the lions is loose!*
  ▸ **free   on the loose**

a
b
c
d
e
f
g
h
i
j
k
l
m
n
o
p
q
r
s
t
u
v
w
x
y
z

lose

a
b
c
d
e
f
g
h
i
j
k
l
m
n
o
p
q
r
s
t
u
v
w
x
y
z

lose *verb*

1 *I've lost my watch.*
▶ to mislay   to misplace
←→ An opposite is **find**.

> **❝ ❞** OTHER WAYS OF SAYING *I've lost my watch.*
> *I can't find my watch.*
> *My watch has gone missing.*

2 *Our team lost the game.*
▶ to be defeated
←→ An opposite is **win**.

lot *noun*

We ate a lot of sweets.
▶ lots   loads

loud *adjective*

1 *We heard a loud explosion.*
▶ noisy   deafening   ear-splitting
2 *I don't like loud music.*
▶ blaring   deafening
3 *He spoke in a loud voice.*
▶ booming   shrill
←→ An opposite is **quiet**.

love *verb*

1 *She loves her sister.*
▶ to be very fond of *She is very fond of her sister.*
to adore (*to love a lot*)
2 *Sam loves his granddad!*
▶ to worship   to idolize
3 *Do you love your boyfriend?*
▶ to be in love with *Are you in love with your boyfriend?*
4 *He loves football!*
▶ to like a lot *He likes football a lot.*
to be very keen on *He is very keen on football.*
to be obsessed with *He is obsessed with football!*

▶▶

5 *I love chocolate!*
- ▶ **to like a lot** *I like chocolate a lot.*
  to adore *I adore chocolate.*
  to be very fond of *I am very fond of chocolate.*
- ← → An opposite is **hate**.

lovely *adjective*

> **!!!** **lovely** *is a word that is often overused.*
>
> 1 *That's a lovely jumper.*
> - ▶ **pretty beautiful**
> 2 *You look lovely in that dress.*
> - ▶ **pretty beautiful attractive glamorous gorgeous stunning**
> 3 *What a lovely painting!*
> - ▶ **nice beautiful gorgeous wonderful**
> 4 *The food was lovely.*
> - ▶ **delicious tasty**
> 5 *The flowers smell lovely.*
> - ▶ **pleasant fragrant perfumed**
> 6 *He's a lovely boy.*
> - ▶ **kind pleasant charming polite**
> 7 *It was a lovely day for sports day.*
> - ▶ **beautiful warm sunny glorious wonderful**
> 8 *We had a lovely time on holiday.*
> - ▶ **enjoyable wonderful fantastic**
> - ← → An opposite is **horrible**.

Low *adjective*

1 *We sat on a low bench.*
- ▶ **small**
2 *Their prices are usually quite low.*
- ▶ **reasonable reduced**
3 *He spoke in a low voice.*
- ▶ **soft deep**
- ← → An opposite is **high**.

Lower *verb*

We lowered the boat into the water.
- ▶ **to drop**

a b c d e f g h i j k l m n o p q r s t u v w x y z

loyal *adjective*
He has many loyal supporters.
▶ devoted   faithful

luck *noun*
It was just by luck that we arrived at the same time.
▶ chance   accident   coincidence

> " " OTHER WAYS OF SAYING *We had good luck.*
> We were lucky.
> We were fortunate.
> We had a stroke of luck.
>
> OTHER WAYS OF SAYING *We had bad luck.*
> We were unlucky.
> We were unfortunate.

lucky *adjective*
We were lucky that we got home before the rain started.
▶ fortunate
◀ ▶ An opposite is **unlucky**.

luggage *noun*
We put all our luggage on the train.
▶ bags   suitcases   baggage

lump *noun*
1 She gave him some bread and a lump of cheese.
▶ a piece   a chunk   a block
2 I've got a lump on my head where I hit it.
▶ a bump   a swelling

machine *noun*
They have a special machine for cutting the metal.
▶ an appliance   a contraption   a tool   a robot

mad *adjective*
1 *I think you're mad if you go outside in this rain!*
▶ crazy   silly   stupid
2 *My mum was really mad with me.*
▶ angry   cross   furious   livid

magic *noun*
1 *He says he can use magic to make it rain.*
▶ sorcery   witchcraft   wizardry
2 *The conjuror did some magic.*
▶ conjuring   tricks

magician *noun*
1 *He was taken prisoner by an evil magician.*
▶ a wizard   a sorcerer   an enchanter
2 *The children watched the magician doing magic tricks.*
▶ a conjuror

magnificent *adjective*
The king lived in a magnificent palace.
▶ grand   splendid   wonderful

mail *noun*
We didn't get any mail this morning.
▶ post   letters   parcels

main *adjective*
The main ingredient of bread is flour.
▶ most important   principal   chief

make verb

1 *I like making model aeroplanes.*
   ▶ to build   to construct   to create
2 *We managed to make a shelter out of some old pieces of wood.*
   ▶ to rig up   to put together
3 *They make cars in that factory.*
   ▶ to produce   to manufacture   to assemble
4 *The heat of the sun can be used to make electricity.*
   ▶ to produce   to generate
5 *We made some cakes and biscuits for the party.*
   ▶ to bake   to cook   to prepare
6 *Hold hands and make a circle.*
   ▶ to form
7 *You can make this old dish into a bird bath.*
   ▶ to change   to turn   to transform
8 *Please don't make too much mess.*
   ▶ to create   to cause
9 *They made me clean the floor.*
   ▶ to force *They forced me to clean the floor.*
     to order *They ordered me to clean the floor.*

man noun

I'll ask the man in the ticket office.
   ▶ a gentleman   a bloke   a guy   a chap
     a bachelor (*an unmarried man*)
     a husband (*a married man*)
     a father (*a man who has children*)
     a widower (*a man whose wife has died*)

manage verb

1 *I finally managed to open the door.*
   ▶ to succeed in *I finally succeeded in opening the door.*
2 *His father manages a shop.*
   ▶ to run   to be in charge of

map noun

He drew a map to show us how to get to the school.
   ▶ a plan   a diagram

mark *noun*

1 *His hands left dirty marks on the wall.*
▶ a stain   a spot   a smear   a smudge   a streak
2 *He had a red mark on his face.*
▶ a spot   a scar   a bruise   a birthmark
His feet had left deep marks in the snow.
▶ footprints   tracks

market *noun*

You can buy all sorts of things at the market.
▶ a bazaar   a street market   a car boot sale

marsh *noun*

We began to sink into the marsh.
▶ a bog   a swamp

marvellous *adjective*

We had a marvellous holiday.
▶ wonderful   brilliant   great   fantastic   perfect

mash *verb*

This machine will mash anything you put into it.
▶ to crush   to squash   to flatten   to grind up   to pulp

mass *noun*

1 *There was a mass of rubbish to clear away.*
▶ a heap   a pile   a mound   a stack
2 *There was a mass of people in front of the stage.*
▶ a group   a crowd   a horde

massive *adjective*

They live in a massive house.
▶ enormous   huge   gigantic   colossal   immense
←→ An opposite is **tiny**.

match *noun*

1 *We watched a football match on TV.*
▶ a game

2 *We went to see a boxing match.*
▶ a contest   a fight

match *verb*
Those socks don't match.
▶ to go together

material *noun*

1 *Stone is a good building material.*
▶ a substance

2 *Her skirt was made of bright yellow material.*
▶ cloth   fabric

• • • SOME TYPES OF MATERIAL

corduroy	cotton	denim	linen	nylon
polyester	satin	silk	velvet	wool

---

maths *noun*
I'm not very good at maths.
▶ mathematics   sums   arithmetic   addition   subtraction
  multiplication   division

matter *noun*

1 *We have an important matter to discuss.*
▶ a subject   a question   an issue

2 *What's the matter?*

❝ ❞ OTHER WAYS OF SAYING *What's the matter?*
What's wrong?
What's the problem?

---

maybe *adverb*
Maybe they'll come later.
▶ perhaps   possibly
◀ ▶ An opposite is **definitely**.

meal noun

SOME TYPES OF MEAL

••• SOME TYPES OF MEAL
breakfast   brunch   dinner
lunch   tea   supper
a feast (*a big meal*)
a snack (*a small meal*)
a picnic (*a meal outside*)
a barbecue (*a meal that you cook outside*)

mean adjective

1 *That was a really mean thing to do.*
  ▶ unkind nasty cruel vindictive
  ←→ An opposite is **kind**.

2 *He's really mean with his money.*
  ▶ stingy tight-fisted miserly
  ←→ An opposite is **generous**.

measurement noun

We wrote down the measurements of the room.
  ▶ the size the dimensions the length the width
  the breadth the height the depth

meat noun

••• SOME TYPES OF MEAT
bacon   beef   chicken   duck
ham   lamb   pork   turkey
venison

medium adjective

I am medium height for my age.
  ▶ average normal ordinary

meet verb

1 *We'll meet at the swimming pool.*
  ▶ to meet up to get together

2 *She will meet us later.*
  ▶ to join to see

3 *I met some of my friends in town.*
  ▶ to see to bump into to run into

▶▶

meeting

4 *I haven't met our new neighbours yet.*
▶ **to be introduced to** *I haven't been introduced to them yet.*
to get to know *I haven't got to know them yet.*
5 *Two rivers meet here.*
▶ **to join   to come together   to merge   to converge**

meeting *noun*
The teachers are having a meeting in the staff room.
▶ **a gathering   a discussion   a conference**

melt *verb*
The ice melted in the sun.
▶ **to thaw   to soften   to unfreeze**

mend *verb*
1 *Do you think you can mend my CD player?*
▶ **to repair   to fix   to put right**
2 *Dad likes mending old furniture.*
▶ **to do up   to restore   to renovate**
3 *I need to mend these jeans.*
▶ **to sew up   to patch**

mention *verb*
1 *Nobody mentioned the stolen money.*
▶ **to talk about   to refer to   to allude to**
2 *She mentioned that the house looked very untidy.*
▶ **to say   to remark**

mercy *noun*
They begged the king to show mercy.
▶ **pity   kindness   compassion   forgiveness**

merry *adjective*
They sang a merry song.
▶ **happy   cheerful   joyful   jolly**
←→ An opposite is **sad**.

mess *noun*

1 *Who's going to clear up all this mess?*
▶ **clutter   untidiness**

2 *The papers were all in a terrible mess.*
▶ **a muddle   a jumble**

message *noun*

She sent me a message to say that she was ill.
▶ **a letter   a note   an email   a text message**

messy *adjective*

The room was very messy.
▶ **untidy   cluttered   dirty   disorganized**
←→ An opposite is **neat**.

metal *noun*

••• SOME TYPES OF METAL			
aluminium	**brass**	**bronze**	**copper**
gold	**iron**	**silver**	**steel**

middle *noun*

1 *There was a big puddle in the middle of the playground.*
▶ **the centre**

2 *They live right in the middle of London.*
▶ **the centre   the heart**

3 *Is it possible to dig right through to the middle of the earth?*
▶ **the core   the centre**

mild *adjective*

1 *The soup had a mild flavour.*
▶ **delicate   subtle   bland**

2 *It was only a mild illness.*
▶ **slight**

3 *The weather was quite mild.*
▶ **warm   calm   pleasant   balmy**

mind

mind *noun*
She's quite old, but her mind is still very active.
▶ brain   memory

mind *verb*
1 Do you mind if I switch the light on?
▶ to object
2 I don't mind if the match is cancelled.
▶ to care
to be bothered *I'm not bothered if the match is cancelled.*

minute *noun*
Please could you wait a minute?
▶ a moment   a second

miserable *adjective*
I felt really miserable when all my friends left.
▶ sad   unhappy   depressed   gloomy   wretched
◀ ▶ An opposite is **cheerful**.

miss *verb*
1 She stepped out into the road and a car just missed her.
▶ to avoid
2 I tried to catch the ball, but I missed it.
▶ to drop
3 Hurry, or you'll miss the bus.
▶ to be late for
4 I really missed my brother when he was away.
▶ to long for   to pine for
5 I missed out two of the questions in the test.
▶ to leave out   to omit

missing *adjective*
Some of the money was still missing.
▶ lost   nowhere to be found *The money was nowhere to be found.*

mist *noun*
They got lost in the mist.
▶ fog   haze

mistake *noun*

1 *I knew I had made a terrible mistake.*
  ▶ **a blunder**
2 *My name had been missed off the list because of a mistake.*
  ▶ **a slip-up   an oversight**
3 *There must be a mistake in your calculations.*
  ▶ **an error   an inaccuracy**
4 *The teacher corrected all the mistakes in my story.*
  ▶ **a spelling mistake   a misspelling**

mix *verb*

1 *Mix red and yellow paint together to make orange.*
  ▶ **to blend   to combine**
2 *Mix all the ingredients together in a bowl.*
  ▶ **to stir   to blend   to beat   to whisk**

mixture *noun*

1 *She dipped her finger into the cake mixture.*
  ▶ **a mix**
2 *We made up a mixture of blue and yellow paint.*
  ▶ **a blend   a combination**
3 *We had sausages with a mixture of different vegetables.*
  ▶ **a variety   an assortment**

moan *verb*

1 *He moaned with pain.*
  ▶ **to groan   to wail**
2 *I wish you would stop moaning about everything!*
  ▶ **to complain   to grumble   to whinge**

model *noun*

They made a model of the Titanic.
  ▶ **a copy   a replica**

modern *adjective*

1 *She likes to wear very modern clothes.*
  ▶ **fashionable   trendy   stylish**
2 *The factory is full of very modern machinery.*
  ▶ **new   up-to-date   futuristic**
3 *He likes listening to modern music.*
  ▶ **contemporary**
  ← → An opposite is **old-fashioned**.

a
b
c
d
e
f
g
h
i
j
k
l
m
n
o
p
q
r
s
t
u
v
w
x
y
z

modest

modest *adjective*

1 *She was very modest about all her achievements.*
▶ **humble self-effacing**
←→ An opposite is **conceited**.

2 *He was too modest to undress on the beach.*
▶ **shy bashful coy**

moment *noun*

Could you just wait a moment?
▶ **a minute a second an instant**

money *noun*

1 *I haven't got enough money to pay for the ice creams.*
▶ **cash change**

2 *There was some money lying on the table.*
▶ **coins silver coppers notes currency**

3 *Some pop stars have got plenty of money.*
▶ **wealth riches**

4 *He earns money by working in a hospital.*
▶ **wages a salary an income pay**

5 *My parents give me money every week.*
▶ **pocket money an allowance**

6 *Have you got any money in the bank?*
▶ **savings funds**

monster *noun*

Focus on **monster**

A huge monster was coming towards them.
▶ **a beast a creature**

SOME TYPES OF MONSTER

a dragon	a giant	an ogre	a troll
a vampire	a werewolf		

SOME WORDS YOU MIGHT USE TO DESCRIBE A MONSTER

huge	ugly	hideous	horrible
terrible	fierce	fearsome	ferocious
terrifying	hairy	scaly	

mood *noun*
Anita seems to be in a very good mood today.
► **humour   temper**

> **" "** OTHER WAYS OF SAYING *She is in a good mood.*
> *She is happy.*
> *She is cheerful.*
> *She's in high spirits.*
>
> OTHER WAYS OF SAYING *She is in a bad mood.*
> *She is sulking.*
> *She is in a huff.*
> *She is moody.*
> *She's down in the dumps.*

moody *adjective*
Why are you so moody today?
► **bad-tempered   sulky   grumpy   irritable   sullen**
←→ An opposite is **cheerful**.

more *adjective*
We need some more money.
► **extra   additional**

mountain *noun*
We could see the mountains in the distance.
► **a hill   a peak**
a mountain range (*a group of mountains*)
a volcano

move *verb*

> **!!!** **move** is a word that is often overused.
>
> **1** *We moved the table into the corner of the room.*
> ► **to push   to pull   to drag   to carry**
> **2** *Please will you move this rubbish.*
> ► **to take away   to carry away   to remove**
> **3** *He sat in the corner and refused to move.*
> ► **to budge   to shift   to change places**
> **4** *The sails were moving in the wind.*
> ► **to stir   to sway   to wave   to flap   to shake** ▶▶

a b c d e f g h i j k l **m** n o p q r s t u v w x y z

move verb (continued)

> **!!!** **move** is a word that is often overused.

> **5** The train was moving quickly through the countryside.
> ▶ to travel to rush to speed to race to cruise
> to hurtle to whizz to zoom
>
> **6** The lorry moved slowly along the road.
> ▶ to crawl to trundle to chug to bump
>
> **7** The skaters moved gracefully over the ice.
> ▶ to glide to slide to skate to slip to float to drift
>
> **8** They moved forwards, towards the building.
> ▶ to advance to proceed to press on
>
> **9** They moved back, away from the fire.
> ▶ to retreat to draw back to withdraw
>
> **10** The plane moved slowly upwards.
> ▶ to rise to climb to ascend
>
> **11** The helicopter moved slowly downwards.
> ▶ to fall to descend to drop to sink
>
> **12** The sign was moving round and round.
> ▶ to spin to turn to rotate to revolve to twirl
> to whirl

mud noun
His boots were covered in mud.
▶ dirt muck clay sludge

muddle noun
My school books were in a terrible muddle.
▶ a mess a jumble

muddle verb
Try not to muddle up the two piles of books.
▶ to jumble up to mix up

murder verb
A gunman murdered the president.
▶ to kill to assassinate

music noun

> ••• SOME TYPES OF MUSIC
>
> | blues | classical | country |
> |-------|-----------|---------|
> | folk | jazz | opera |
> | pop | reggae | rock |

musical instrument noun

> ••• SOME STRINGED INSTRUMENTS
>
> | a banjo | a cello | a double |
> |---------|---------|----------|
> | bassa guitar | a harp | a mandolin |
> | a sitar | a viola | a violin |
>
> SOME WOODWIND INSTRUMENTS
>
> | a bassoon | a clarinet | a flute |
> |-----------|------------|---------|
> | an oboe | a piccolo | a recorder |
>
> SOME BRASS INSTRUMENTS
>
> | a bugle | a cornet | a horn |
> |---------|----------|--------|
> | a saxophone | a trombone | a trumpet |
> | a tuba | | |
>
> SOME KEYBOARD INSTRUMENTS
>
> | an accordion | a harpsichord | a keyboard |
> |--------------|---------------|------------|
> | an organ | a piano | |
>
> SOME PERCUSSION INSTRUMENTS
>
> | cymbals | a drum | |
> |---------|--------|--------|
> | a glockenspiel | a tambourine | a triangle |
> | a xylophone | | |

musician noun

Would you like to be a professional musician?

▶ a performer a player a singer a composer

mysterious adjective

She disappeared in a very mysterious way.

▶ strange puzzling mystifying

mystery noun

The police finally solved the mystery.

▶ a puzzle a riddle

Nn

naked *adjective*
The baby was naked.
▶ bare nude unclothed
◄ ➤ An opposite is **dressed**.

name *noun*
What is your name?
▶ a first name a surname a family name a nickname

narrow *adjective*
We walked along a narrow path.
▶ thin slim
◄ ➤ An opposite is **broad**.

nasty *adjective*
1 *He's a very nasty boy.*
▶ horrible unpleasant mean spiteful unkind obnoxious horrid
2 *There was a nasty smell in the kitchen.*
▶ horrible unpleasant revolting disgusting foul
3 *He's got a nasty cut on his arm.*
▶ bad awful terrible painful
◄ ➤ An opposite is **nice**.

natural *adjective*
1 *This jumper is made of natural wool.*
▶ real genuine pure
◄ ➤ An opposite is **artificial**.
2 *It's natural to feel upset when your pet dies.*
▶ normal ordinary usual
◄ ➤ An opposite is **unnatural**.

naughty *adjective*
Have you ever been naughty?
▶ bad badly behaved disobedient mischievous disruptive bad-mannered rude
◄ ➤ An opposite is **well-behaved**.

near *adjective*
Our house is near the school.
▶ close to   next to   beside

nearly *adverb*
I've nearly finished.
▶ almost   virtually   just about   practically

neat *adjective*
1 Her bedroom is always very neat.
  ▶ tidy   clean   orderly   spick and span
2 He looked very neat in his new uniform.
  ▶ smart   elegant   well-turned-out
← → An opposite is **untidy**.

necessary *adjective*
It is necessary to water plants in dry weather.
  ▶ important   essential   vital
← → An opposite is **unnecessary**.

need *verb*
1 All plants and animals need water.
  ▶ to require   to depend on   to rely on
2 Do you need any more money?
  ▶ to require   to want   t
  o be short of Are you short of money?
3 You need to tidy your room.
  ▶ to have to You have to tidy your room.
  should You should tidy your room.
  must You must tidy your room.
  ought to You ought to tidy your room.

nervous *adjective*
1 Are you nervous about starting your new school?
  ▶ worried   anxious   apprehensive
2 The horses seemed very nervous.
  ▶ jumpy   agitated   fearful   panicky
← → An opposite is **calm**.

neutral *adjective*
The referee has to be neutral.
  ▶ fair   impartial   unbiased

new *adjective*

1 *She was wearing a new dress.*
  ▶ **brand new**
2 *The hospital has got a lot of new equipment.*
  ▶ **modern up-to-date state-of-the-art**
3 *We're moving to a new house.*
  ▶ **different**
4 *See if you can think of some new ideas.*
  ▶ **fresh different novel innovative**
  ← → An opposite is **old**.

next *adjective*

1 *They live in the next street.*
  ▶ **nearest closest adjacent**
2 *They set off the next day.*
  ▶ **following**

nice *adjective*

!!! **nice** is a word that is often overused.

1 *That's a nice dress.*
  ▶ **pretty lovely beautiful stylish**
2 *You look very nice with your hair short.*
  ▶ **pretty beautiful handsome lovely smart
  attractive gorgeous glamorous stunning**
3 *That's a very nice picture.*
  ▶ **lovely beautiful gorgeous wonderful**
4 *The food was very nice.*
  ▶ **delicious tasty**
5 *Some of the flowers smell very nice.*
  ▶ **pleasant fragrant perfumed**
6 *Did you have a nice holiday?*
  ▶ **pleasant lovely enjoyable wonderful fantastic**
7 *He's a very nice boy.*
  ▶ **friendly kind thoughtful likeable pleasant
  charming polite**
8 *I hope we have nice weather for our trip to the beach.*
  ▶ **lovely pleasant beautiful warm sunny glorious
  wonderful**
  ← → An opposite is **horrible**.

noise *noun*

1 *Stop that noise!*
   ▶ din   racket   row   rumpus   uproar
2 *Suddenly, I heard a loud noise.*
   ▶ a sound   a bang   a clatter   a thud   a thump   a roar
   a rumble   a clang   a clank   a scream   a shout   a screech
   a squeak

noisy *adjective*

1 *The band's music was very noisy.*
   ▶ loud   deafening   ear-splitting
2 *She asked the children not to be so noisy.*
   ▶ loud   rowdy   boisterous
← → An opposite is **quiet**.

nonsense *noun*

Don't talk nonsense!
   ▶ rubbish   drivel

normal *adjective*

1 *It's quite normal to feel tired at the end of the day.*
   ▶ natural   common   usual
2 *It looked like a normal car.*
   ▶ ordinary   standard   typical
← → An opposite is **abnormal**.

normally *adverb*

I normally go to bed at eight o'clock.
   ▶ usually   generally

nosy *adjective*

Don't be so nosy!
   ▶ inquisitive   snooping   prying   curious

note *noun*

I found a note saying that he would be home for tea.
   ▶ a letter   a message   a reminder

a
b
c
d
e
f
g
h
i
j
k
l
m
n
o
p
q
r
s
t
u
v
w
x
y
z

notice

a

b

notice *noun*

We put up a notice to tell people about our play.

▶ a poster   a sign   an announcement   an advertisement

notice *verb*

I noticed that there were no lights on in the house.

▶ to observe   to see   to spot

nuisance *noun*

1 *That dog is a nuisance!*

▶ a pest   a bother   a pain

2 *The rain was a nuisance.*

▶ a problem   an irritation   an inconvenience

number *noun*

Can you add up those numbers?

▶ a figure   a digit

a
b
c
d
e
f
g
h
i
j
k
l
m
n
o
p
q
r
s
t
u
v
w
x
y
z

obey *verb*
You must obey the rules.
> ▶ **to abide by** *You must abide by the rules.*
> **to not break** *You must not break the rules.*
> ←→ An opposite is **disobey**.

object *noun*
We found some interesting objects in the cupboard.
> ▶ **a thing   an article   an item**

object *verb*
Some people object to violence in films.
> ▶ **to not like** *Some people do not like violence.*
> **to complain about   to disapprove of**
> **to be opposed to** *Some people are opposed to violence.*

obvious *adjective*
It was obvious that he was lying.
> ▶ **clear   plain   apparent   evident**

occasionally *adverb*
We occasionally go swimming.
> ▶ **sometimes   from time to time   now and then**

odd *adjective*
It seemed odd that the school was so quiet.
> ▶ **strange   funny   peculiar   curious**
> ←→ An opposite is **normal**.

offer *verb*
1 *She offered me a piece of cake.*
> ▶ **to give   to hand**
2 *Tom offered to wash up.*
> ▶ **to volunteer**

a
b
c
d
e
f
g
h
i
j
k
l
m
n
o
p
q
r
s
t
u
v
w
x
y
z

often *adverb*
We often go swimming on Saturdays.
  ▸ frequently   regularly

old *adjective*
  1 *My grandmother is quite old.*
    ▸ elderly   aged
    ←→ An opposite is **young**.
  2 *Our car is getting quite old now.*
    ▸ ancient   old-fashioned
    ←→ An opposite is **modern**.
  3 *We threw out all the old newspapers.*
    ▸ out-of-date
    ←→ An opposite is **new**.
  4 *Wear old clothes when you are painting.*
    ▸ tatty   shabby   scruffy   worn-out
    ←→ An opposite is **new**.
  5 *Old furniture can often be valuable.*
    ▸ antique

open *adjective*
Someone had left the door open.
  ▸ ajar   wide open   unlocked   unfastened
  ←→ An opposite is **closed**.

open *verb*
  1 *He opened the door.*
    ▸ to unlock   to push open   to fling open   to throw open
      to break down (*to open by breaking it*)
  2 *The door opened.*
    ▸ to burst open   to fly open   to swing open
  3 *He opened the car window.*
    ▸ to wind down   to roll down
  ←→ An opposite is **close**.

opening *noun*
We crawled through an opening in the fence.
  ▸ a gap   a hole   a space

opinion *noun*
What's your opinion about what happened?
► an idea   a belief   a view

opposite *adjective*
1 *The live on the opposite side of the road.*
► facing
2 *North is the opposite direction to south.*
► different   opposing

order *noun*
You must obey my orders.
► a command   an instruction

order *verb*
1 *He ordered us to stand still.*
► to tell   to command   to instruct
2 *We ordered some sandwiches and drinks.*
► to ask for   to request   to send for

ordinary *adjective*
1 *It was just an ordinary day.*
► normal   usual   typical   everyday   unexciting
2 *It's just an ordinary house.*
► normal   standard   average
← → An opposite is **special**.

organize *verb*
Our teacher organized a trip to the zoo.
► to arrange   to plan   to set up

original *adjective*
1 *Try to think of some original ideas.*
► new   fresh   imaginative
2 *The original version has been lost.*
► first   earliest   initial

a
b
c
d
e
f
g
h
i
j
k
l
m
n
o
p
q
r
s
t
u
v
w
x
y
z

outing *noun*
We went on an outing to the country park.
▶ a trip   an excursion   an expedition

overgrown *adjective*
The garden was very overgrown.
▶ untidy   weedy   tangled

own *verb*
Do you own a bike?
▶ to have   to possess

own *adjective*
I have my own guitar.
▶ personal   private

own up *verb*
He owned up to stealing the money.
▶ to admit *He admitted stealing the money.*
to confess *He confessed to stealing the money.*

pack *verb*

We packed everything into the car.
▶ to put   to load   to stow   to cram

packed *adjective*

The cinema was packed with people.
▶ full   crowded   jam-packed

packet *noun*

I bought a packet of cornflakes.
▶ a box   a pack   a carton

page *noun*

There's a lovely picture on the next page.
▶ a sheet   a side

pain *noun*

1 *I've got a pain in my stomach.*
▶ an ache

> **❝ ❞** ANOTHER WAY OF SAYING *I've got a pain in my stomach.*
> *My stomach hurts.*

2 *I felt a sudden pain in my leg.*
▶ a twinge   a pang
3 *She was in terrible pain.*
▶ agony

painful *adjective*

Is your knee still painful?
▶ sore   hurting   aching   tender

paint *verb*

We're going to paint my bedroom during the holidays.
▶ to decorate   to redecorate

pale *adjective*

1 *She looked very tired and pale.*
▶ white   white-faced   pallid

2 *He was wearing a pale blue shirt.*
▶ light

←→ An opposite is **bright**.

pant *verb*

He was panting by the time he reached the top of the hill.
▶ to gasp   to gasp for breath   to puff   to huff and puff

paper *noun*

1 *He wrote his name on a piece of paper.*
▶ notepaper   writing paper   card

2 *The cups were all wrapped in paper.*
▶ tissue paper   wrapping paper

3 *I read a paper every day.*
▶ a newspaper   a tabloid   a broadsheet

parcel *noun*

There's a parcel for you!
▶ a package   a packet

part *noun*

1 *He kept a small part of the cake for himself.*
▶ a bit   a piece   a portion

2 *I didn't like the last part of the story.*
▶ a bit   a section

3 *We have completed the first part of our journey.*
▶ a stage   a phase

4 *We live in a very nice part of the country.*
▶ an area   a region

5 *Which part of the city do you live in?*
▶ an area   a district

particular *adjective*

1 *There was one particular dress that she liked.*
▶ specific   special

2 *She has her own particular way of writing.*
▶ individual   personal   special   unique

partner *noun*

1 *Choose a partner to work with.*
▶ a friend   a companion   a colleague   a helper

party *noun*

Are you having a party?
▶ a birthday party   a celebration   a gathering   a disco
a dance

pass *verb*

1 *I pass this shop every day on my way to school.*
▶ to go past   to go by

2 *We passed an old van on the motorway.*
▶ to overtake

3 *Could you pass me the salt, please?*
▶ to hand   to give

passage *noun*

1 *We walked down a narrow passage to the kitchen.*
▶ a corridor   a passageway

2 *They say there's a secret passage under the castle.*
▶ a tunnel   a walkway

pat *verb*

He patted the dog on the head.
▶ to touch   to stroke   to tap

path *noun*

We walked along the path.
▶ a footpath   a track
a bridleway (*a path for horses*)

patient *adjective*

It won't take very long, so please be patient.
▶ calm   tolerant
←→ An opposite is **impatient**.

pattern *noun*

She was wearing a blue dress with a white pattern on.
▶ a design

a
b
c
d
e
f
g
h
i
j
k
l
m
n
o
p
q
r
s
t
u
v
w
x
y
z

a
b
c
d
e
f
g
h
i
j
k
l
m
n
o
p
q
r
s
t
u
v
w
x
y
z

pause *verb*
He paused before opening the door.
> ▶ to stop to wait to hesitate

pay *noun*
You will get your pay at the end of the week.
> ▶ wages salary

pay *verb*
1 *He paid a lot of money for that bike.*
> ▶ to give to spend
> to fork out *He forked out a lot of money on that bike.*
2 *If you let me have the video now, I'll pay you tomorrow.*
> ▶ to repay to reimburse

peace *noun*
1 *After the war ended there was peace between the two countries.*
> ▶ friendliness an agreement a truce
2 *We sat by the lake and enjoyed the peace of the evening.*
> ▶ quiet peacefulness calmness stillness

peaceful *adjective*
It seemed very peaceful when the baby had gone to sleep.
> ▶ quiet calm tranquil
← → An opposite is **noisy**.

peculiar *adjective*
This ice cream has a peculiar taste.
> ▶ strange funny odd curious bizarre
← → An opposite is **normal**.

pen *noun*

••• SOME TYPES OF PEN		
a ballpoint pen	a Biro™	a felt-tip pen
a fountain pen	a quill (*an old-fashioned pen*)	
a rollerball		

people *noun*
1 *The streets were full of people.*
▶ **folk men and women**
2 *People are not allowed on this private beach.*
▶ **the public**
3 *The president was elected by the people of his country.*
▶ **the population the citizens**

perfect *adjective*
1 *It's a perfect day for a picnic.*
▶ **ideal excellent**
2 *This is a perfect piece of work.*
▶ **excellent flawless faultless**
3 *The dress was a perfect fit.*
▶ **exact**

perform *verb*
1 *The children performed the play in front of their parents.*
▶ **to put on to present**
2 *I don't like performing in public.*
▶ **to act to dance to sing to be on stage**

perfume *noun*
We bought Mum some perfume for her birthday.
▶ **scent**

perhaps *adverb*
Perhaps we'll see you tomorrow.
▶ **maybe possibly**

person *noun*
1 *I saw a person walking towards me.*
▶ **a man a woman an adult a grown-up a child a teenager a boy a girl**
2 *He's a very unpleasant person.*
▶ **an individual a character a human being**

personal *adjective*
She's got her own personal mug.
▶ **special individual private**

a
b
c
d
e
f
g
h
i
j
k
l
m
n
o
p
q
r
s
t
u
v
w
x
y
z

personality

personality *noun*
She's got a lovely personality.
▶ a character   a nature   a temperament

persuade *verb*
She persuaded her mum to take her swimming.
▶ to urge   to encourage
to talk someone into *She talked her mum into taking her swimming.*

pester *verb*
My little brother kept pestering me.
▶ to annoy   to bother   to harass   to hassle

phone *verb*
I phoned my grandma to ask how she was.
▶ to call   to ring   to telephone
to give someone a ring *I gave my grandma a ring.*

photograph *noun*
I took a photograph of my sister.
▶ a photo   a picture   a shot   a snapshot

pick *verb*
1 *I didn't know which cake to pick.*
▶ to choose   to select   to decide on
2 *We picked some blackberries for tea.*
▶ to gather   to collect   to harvest
3 *She picked a flower from the bush.*
▶ to pluck   to cut
4 *She picked the book up off the floor.*
▶ to lift up

picture *noun*
1 *There was a picture of a lion on the wall.*
▶ a drawing   a painting   a sketch   a photograph   a print
2 *We found an old picture of my grandfather.*
▶ a painting   a portrait
3 *Are there any pictures in this book?*
▶ an illustration   an image
4 *Someone had drawn a funny picture of the teacher.*
▶ a cartoon   a caricature

piece *noun*

1 *She gave me a huge piece of cake.*
▶ **a bit   a slice   a sliver   a wedge** (*a thick slice*)

2 *Would you like a piece of chocolate?*
▶ **a bit   a square   a chunk**

3 *He cut off a piece of cheese.*
▶ **a bit   a lump   a chunk**

4 *We need another piece of wood.*
▶ **a bit   a block   a plank**

5 *She handed me a piece of paper.*
▶ **a bit   a sheet   a scrap** (*a small piece*)

6 *We need a new piece of glass for that window.*
▶ **a sheet   a pane**

7 *A huge piece of concrete fell off the building.*
▶ **a block   a slab**

8 *Mum told Jo to pick up every single piece of the broken cup.*
▶ **a bit   a chip   a fragment**

9 *I need a piece of cloth to clean my bike.*
▶ **a scrap**

pierce *verb*
The knight's sword pierced the dragon's thick skin.
▶ **to prick   to penetrate   to go through   to puncture**

pig *noun*
▶ **a hog**
a boar (*a male pig*)
a sow (*a female pig*)
a piglet (*a baby pig*)

pile *noun*
There was a pile of dirty clothes on the floor.
▶ **a heap   a mound   a mass   a stack**

pillar *noun*
The roof was held up by large pillars.
▶ **a column   a post   a support**

pipe *noun*
There was water coming out of the pipe.
▶ **a hose   a tube**

pity noun

1 *She felt great pity for the hungry children.*
► **sympathy   understanding**

2 *The soldiers showed no pity to their enemies.*
► **mercy   kindness   compassion**

3 *It's a pity you can't come to the party.*
► **a shame**

> 6 9 ANOTHER WAY OF SAYING *It's a pity you can't come.*
> *It's unfortunate that you can't come.*

place noun

1 *A cross marks the place where the treasure is buried.*
► **a spot   a position   a point   a location   a site**

2 *Our school is in a very nice place.*
► **an area   a district   a neighbourhood   a town   a city
   a village**

3 *Save me a place next to you.*
► **a chair   a seat**

place verb

FOR OTHER VERBS, SEE put

plain adjective

The food in the hotel was quite plain.
► **ordinary   simple   not fancy   dull**

plan noun

1 *He has a secret plan to get the money back.*
► **an idea   a scheme   a plot**

2 *We drew a plan of the town to show where we all live.*
► **a map   a diagram   a chart**

3 *I made a plan for my story.*
► **a framework   a structure**

plan verb

1 *When do you plan to leave?*
► **to intend   to aim**

2 *He thinks they are planning to rob a bank.*
► **to plot   to scheme**

3 *We need to plan this trip very carefully.*
► **to organize   to arrange   to prepare for**

plane *noun*
SEE **aeroplane**

plant *noun*
The garden is full of beautiful plants.

• • • SOME TYPES OF PLANT

a bulb	a bush	a cactus	a fern
a flower	a herb	a shrub	a tree
a vegetable	a weed		

---

play *noun*
The children are putting on a play at the end of term.
▶ a show   a performance
a comedy (*a funny play*)
a tragedy (*a sad play*)
a pantomime   a drama

play *verb*
1 The children were playing on the beach.
▶ to have fun *They were having fun.*
to enjoy yourself *They were enjoying themselves.*
to amuse yourself *They were amusing themselves.*
2 She played a tune on the piano.
▶ to perform

playful *adjective*
Kittens can be playful.
▶ lively   mischievous   frisky   fun-loving   cheeky
← → An opposite is **serious**.

pleasant *adjective*
1 We had a very pleasant day on the beach.
▶ nice   lovely   enjoyable   wonderful   fantastic
2 He seems a very pleasant boy.
▶ friendly   kind   thoughtful   likeable   nice   charming
3 The weather was very pleasant.
▶ lovely   nice   beautiful   warm   sunny   glorious   wonderful
← → An opposite is **unpleasant**.

a b c d e f g h i j k l m n o p q r s t u v w x y z

a
b
c
d
e
f
g
h
i
j
k
l
m
n
o
p
q
r
s
t
u
v
w
x
y
z

pleased *adjective*

I was pleased that so many people came to my party.
  ▶ delighted thrilled happy glad grateful thankful chuffed
  ← → An opposite is **annoyed**.

pleasure *noun*

She smiled with pleasure.
  ▶ happiness enjoyment contentment delight joy

plot *verb*

I knew they were plotting to steal the jewels.
  ▶ to plan to scheme

plump *adjective*

1 *The shopkeeper was a small, plump man.*
  ▶ fat stout tubby round pot-bellied portly
2 *On her lap was a plump, smiling baby.*
  ▶ chubby podgy fat
  ← → An opposite is **thin**.

plunge *verb*

She plunged into the water.
  ▶ to jump to leap to dive

poem *noun*

We had to write a poem about the spring.
  ▶ a rhyme a verse a limerick a lyric a sonnet a haiku

point *noun*

1 *Be careful, that knife has got a very sharp point.*
  ▶ an end a tip
2 *We soon reached the point where the two roads met.*
  ▶ a place a spot
3 *At that point I did not know about the treasure.*
  ▶ a time a moment a stage
4 *What is the point of this game?*
  ▶ the purpose the aim the object

point *verb*
1 *He pointed towards the castle.*
▶ to indicate   to gesture towards
2 *I pointed the hose at the paddling pool.*
▶ to aim   to direct

pointed *adjective*
He used a pointed stick to make a hole in the ground.
▶ sharp   sharpened

poisonous *adjective*
1 *Some toadstools are poisonous.*
▶ harmful   deadly   lethal   toxic
2 *She was bitten by a poisonous snake.*
▶ venomous

poke *verb*
1 *He poked the dead mouse with a stick.*
▶ to prod   to push   to jab
2 *She poked me in the back.*
▶ to nudge   to dig   to prod   to elbow

pole *noun*
We tied the flag to a pole.
▶ a post

policeman, policewoman *noun*
There was a policeman at the door.
▶ a police officer   an officer   a constable   a sergeant
an inspector   a detective

polite *adjective*
He's a very polite boy.
▶ well-mannered   well-behaved   respectful
courteous
←→ An opposite is **rude**.

a
b
c
d
e
f
g
h
i
j
k
l
m
n
o
p
q
r
s
t
u
v
w
x
y
z

poor *adjective*

1 *His mother and father were very poor.*
  ▶ **penniless   poverty-stricken   needy   hard up**
  ←→ An opposite is **rich**.

2 *This is very poor work.*
  ▶ **bad   careless   sloppy**
  ←→ An opposite is **good**.

poorly *adjective*

I was poorly yesterday.
  ▶ **ill   unwell   sick**
  ←→ An opposite is **well**.

popular *adjective*

1 *He is a popular TV presenter.*
  ▶ **famous   well-known   well-liked**

2 *Football is a very popular sport.*
  ▶ **well-liked**
  ←→ An opposite is **unpopular**.

> **❝❞** ANOTHER WAY OF SAYING *Football is very popular.*
> *A lot of people like football.*

portion *noun*

1 *She gave me a huge portion of chips.*
  ▶ **a helping   a serving**

2 *I only got a small portion of pie.*
  ▶ **a piece   a slice**

positive *adjective*

I am positive I saw him.
  ▶ **certain   sure   convinced**

possessions *noun*

We lost all our possessions in the fire.
  ▶ **belongings   property   things**

possible *adjective*

It is possible that it will rain later.
  ▶ **likely   conceivable   feasible**
  ←→ An opposite is **impossible**.

post *noun*
1 *The fence is supported by wooden posts.*
 ▶ a pole a stake
2 *Did you get any post this morning?*
 ▶ mail letters parcels

poster *noun*
We put up a poster to tell people about our concert.
 ▶ a notice a sign an announcement an advertisement

postpone *verb*
We had to postpone the match because of the bad weather.
 ▶ to put off to cancel to delay

pour *verb*
1 *I poured some orange juice into a glass.*
 ▶ to tip
2 *Water was pouring over the edge of the bath.*
 ▶ to run to stream to spill to gush to splash
3 *It was pouring with rain.*
 ▶ to teem to pelt down to bucket down

power *noun*
1 *The police have the power to arrest criminals.*
 ▶ the right the authority
2 *In stories, magicians have special powers.*
 ▶ an ability a skill a talent
3 *Many buildings were destroyed by the power of the waves.*
 ▶ force strength might
4 *There is no power left in these batteries.*
 ▶ energy

powerful *adjective*
1 *He was a rich and powerful king.*
 ▶ mighty all-powerful
2 *They used powerful machines to lift the train off the rails.*
 ▶ mighty great
3 *The lion crushed the bones with its powerful jaws.*
 ▶ strong mighty
 ← → An opposite is **weak**.

a b c d e f g h i j k l m n o p q r s t u v w x y z

practise *verb*

1 *I need to practise my speech.*
▶ **to go through   to run through   to work on   to rehearse**

2 *The football team meets once a week to practise.*
▶ **to train**

praise *verb*

Our teacher praised us for working so hard.
▶ **to congratulate   to commend   to compliment**
←→ An opposite is **criticize**.

precious *adjective*

1 *The thieves stole a lot of precious jewellery.*
▶ **valuable   expensive   priceless**

2 *I have a special box for all my precious possessions.*
▶ **prized   treasured   cherished   much-loved**

precise *adjective*

Make sure you measure out the precise amount.
▶ **exact   correct   right   accurate**

prepare *verb*

1 *We are all busy preparing for the party.*
▶ **to get ready   to make preparations   to make arrangements   to plan**

2 *I helped my mum prepare lunch.*
▶ **to make   to cook**
to get ready *I helped my mum get the lunch ready.*

present *noun*

I got some lovely presents for my birthday.
▶ **a gift**

present *verb*

1 *The head presented the prize to the winner.*
▶ **to give   to hand   to award**

2 *Who will present the show tonight?*
▶ **to introduce   to host**

press *verb*

Don't press any of the buttons.
▶ **to push   to touch**

pretend *verb*

1 *I thought she was hurt, but she was only pretending.*
▶ to put it on   to fake   to play-act
2 *Let's pretend we're pirates.*
▶ to imagine   to make believe   to play

pretty *adjective*

1 *You look pretty today.*
▶ lovely   beautiful   attractive
stunning (*very pretty*)
gorgeous
2 *What a pretty little cottage!*
▶ quaint   charming
←→ An opposite is **ugly**.

prevent *verb*

1 *He tried to prevent us from leaving.*
▶ to stop
2 *We must act quickly to prevent an accident.*
▶ to avoid   to avert

price *noun*

1 *What was the price of those trainers?*
▶ the cost
2 *What price do you have to pay to go into the museum?*
▶ a charge   a fee
3 *The bus company is going to increase its prices for all journeys.*
▶ a fare

prick *verb*

I pricked my finger on a needle.
▶ to jab   to stab   to pierce

prison *noun*

The thief was sent to prison for ten years.
▶ jail   a cell   a dungeon

prisoner *noun*

The prisoners were only given bread and water.
▶ a convict   an inmate
a hostage (*a person taken prisoner by a kidnapper*)
a captive

private *adjective*

1 *They have their own private beach.*
▶ personal

2 *You mustn't read her private letters.*
▶ confidential   personal   secret

3 *We found a nice private spot for a picnic.*
▶ hidden   secluded   quiet   isolated

prize *noun*

I hope I win a prize.
▶ an award   a trophy   a cup   a medal

problem *noun*

1 *The lack of food was going to be a problem.*
▶ a difficulty   a worry   trouble

2 *We had some difficult maths problems to solve.*
▶ a question

3 *We solved the problem of the missing shoe.*
▶ a mystery   a riddle   an enigma

prod *verb*

1 *She prodded the worm with a stick.*
▶ to poke   to push   to jab

2 *Someone prodded me in the back.*
▶ to nudge   to dig   to poke   to elbow

produce *verb*

1 *This factory produces furniture.*
▶ to make   to manufacture   to assemble

2 *Farmers produce food for us.*
▶ to grow

3 *She produced a photo from her bag.*
▶ to bring out   to take out

promise *verb*

Do you promise that you will be home by five o'clock?
▶ to give your word   to swear   to vow   to guarantee

proof *noun*

I think she took my pen, but I haven't got any proof.
▶ evidence   facts   information

prop *verb*
> *He propped his bike against the wall.*
>> ▶ **to lean to rest**

proper *adjective*
> **1** *Please put the book back in its proper place.*
>> ▶ **correct right**
> **2** *Can we have a ride in a proper boat?*
>> ▶ **real genuine**

protect *verb*
> **1** *The bird always protects its chicks.*
>> ▶ **to defend to guard to look after**
>> **to keep safe** *She tried to keep them safe.*
> **2** *The hedge protected us from the wind.*
>> ▶ **to shelter to shield**

protest *verb*
> *The children protested when the teacher said they had to stay indoors.*
>> ▶ **to complain to object**

proud *adjective*
> *Her parents felt very proud when she went up to collect her prize.*
>> ▶ **pleased happy delighted**
> ← → An opposite is **ashamed**.

prove *verb*
> *Can you prove that you live here?*
>> ▶ **to show to establish to demonstrate**

provide *verb*
> **1** *Our parents provided us with food for the trip.*
>> ▶ **to supply to give**
> **2** *You will need to provide your own towel.*
>> ▶ **to bring to take**

prowl *verb*
> *The tiger prowled round the tree.*
>> ▶ **to creep to slink**

pry *verb*
You shouldn't pry into other people's business
▶ to interfere   to meddle   to poke your nose in

public *adjective*
This is a public beach, not a private one.
▶ open   communal   shared
←→ An opposite is **private**.

publish *verb*
The school publishes a magazine once a term.
▶ to bring out   to produce   to issue   to print

pudding *noun*
Would you like some pudding?
▶ dessert   sweet

puff *verb*
I was puffing a bit by the time I got to the top of the hill.
▶ to pant   to huff and puff   to gasp   to gasp for breath

pull *verb*
1 *We pulled the heavy box across the floor.*
▶ to drag   to haul   to lug
2 *I got hold of the handle and pulled.*
▶ to tug   to yank   to heave
3 *The magician pulled a bunch of flowers out of a hat.*
▶ to take   to lift   to draw   to bring   to produce
4 *I managed to pull the book out of her hands.*
▶ to tear   to wrench   to drag   to rip
5 *The car was pulling a caravan.*
▶ to tow
6 *The horse was pulling a cart.*
▶ to draw

pull off *verb*
I pulled off the label.
▶ to rip off   to tear off   to break off

punch *verb*
That boy punched me!
▶ to hit   to thump   to wallop   to strike

punish *verb*
The teachers will punish you if you misbehave.
▶ to discipline   to make an example of

pupil *noun*
This school has about five hundred pupils.
▶ a schoolchild   a schoolboy   a schoolgirl   a student

pure *adjective*
1 *He was wearing a crown made of pure gold.*
▶ real   solid
2 *We bought a carton of pure orange juice.*
▶ natural
3 *The water here is lovely and pure.*
▶ clean   fresh   unpolluted

purpose *noun*
What is the purpose of your journey?
▶ the aim   the point   the reason for   the intention

purse *noun*
Always keep your money in a purse.
▶ a wallet   a bag

push *verb*
1 *The door will open if you push harder.*
▶ to press   to shove   to apply pressure
2 *I pushed my key into the lock.*
▶ to stick   to thrust   to ram
3 *I managed to push all the clothes into the bag.*
▶ to force   to stuff   to squeeze   to jam   to cram
4 *We pushed the table into the corner of the room.*
▶ to move   to shove   to drag
5 *We pushed the trolley towards the checkout.*
▶ to wheel   to trundle   to roll
6 *Someone pushed me in the back.*
▶ to shove   to nudge   to prod   to poke   to elbow
7 *The boy pushed past me.*
▶ to shove   to barge   to squeeze   to elbow your way

put

put *verb*

!!! **put** *is a word that is often overused.*

1 *Put all the pencils on my desk.*
▶ to place to pop to leave

2 *Put the books over there.*
▶ to stack to pile

3 *He ran in and put his bag on the floor.*
▶ to drop to dump to deposit to plonk to leave

4 *She put the clock carefully in the middle of the table.*
▶ to place to position to set

5 *I'll put the flowers in a vase.*
▶ to arrange

6 *I put a coin into the slot.*
▶ to slide to insert

7 *He put all the dirty clothes back into his bag.*
▶ to shove to push to stick to bung to stuff

8 *He put some sugar on his cereal.*
▶ to sprinkle to scatter

9 *Can you put some water on these plants?*
▶ to spray to sprinkle to pour

10 *I put some butter on my bread.*
▶ to spread

11 *We put all the pictures on the table so that we could see them.*
▶ to lay to lay out to set out to spread out to arrange

12 *She put her bike against the wall.*
▶ to lean to rest to stand to prop

13 *They have put some new lights on the outside of the school*
▶ to fix to attach to install to fit

14 *You can put your car in the car park.*
▶ to park to leave

put off *verb*
The match has been put off until next week.
▶ to postpone to cancel to delay

put up with *verb*
How can you put up with this noise?
▶ to tolerate   to endure   to live with

puzzle *noun*
1 *I like doing puzzles.*
▶ a brainteaser   a problem
2 *The disappearance of the keys was still a puzzle.*
▶ a mystery   a riddle   an enigma

puzzled *adjective*
I was puzzled when I found the door wide open.
▶ confused   bewildered   baffled   mystified

Qq

quake *verb*
The children were quaking with fear.
▶ to shake to tremble to quiver to shiver to shudder

quality *noun*
The children have produced some work of very high quality.
▶ a standard

quantity *noun*
In hot weather the shop sells a large quantity of ice cream.
▶ an amount

quarrel *verb*
Those two are always quarrelling.
▶ to argue to squabble to fight to fall out to bicker
to disagree

quarrel *noun*
She had a quarrel with her brother.
▶ an argument a disagreement a row a fight

queer *adjective*
The biscuits had a queer taste.
▶ strange funny odd peculiar bizarre
←→ An opposite is **normal**.

question *noun*
There was no one who could answer my question.
▶ a query an enquiry

queue *noun*
1 *There was a long queue of people waiting for ice creams.*
▶ a line
2 *There was a long queue of traffic on the motorway.*
▶ a line a tailback

quick *adjective*

  1 *It was quite a quick journey.*
    ▶ **fast speedy swift**

  2 *He made a quick recovery from his illness.*
    ▶ **rapid speedy instant**

  3 *He was walking at a quick pace.*
    ▶ **brisk fast swift**

  4 *We had a quick lunch and then left.*
    ▶ **speedy hasty hurried brief**

  5 *They only came for a quick visit.*
    ▶ **short brief fleeting**

  6 *I would like a quick reply.*
    ▶ **immediate instant prompt**

quiet *adjective*

  1 *Our teacher told us to be quiet.*
    ▶ **silent**
    ←→ An opposite is **noisy**.

  2 *We found a quiet place for our picnic.*
    ▶ **peaceful isolated tranquil**
    ←→ An opposite is **crowded**.

  3 *She's a very quiet girl.*
    ▶ **reserved placid shy gentle**
    ←→ An opposite is **noisy**.

  4 *I listened to some quiet music.*
    ▶ **low soft**
    ←→ An opposite is **loud**.

quite *adverb*

  1 *The water's quite warm.*
    ▶ **fairly pretty reasonably rather**

  2 *I'm not quite sure.*
    ▶ **completely totally absolutely**

a
b
c
d
e
f
g
h
i
j
k
l
m
n
o
p
q
r
s
t
u
v
w
x
y
z

a b c d e f g h i j k l m n o p q **r** s t u v w x y z

rain *noun*

Focus on **rain**

> *There could be some rain later.*
> ▶ a shower
> drizzle (*very light rain*)
> a downpour (*heavy rain*)
> a storm

SOME WORDS YOU MIGHT USE TO DESCRIBE RAIN
fine	light	gentle	steady
heavy	torrential		

SOME WORDS YOU MIGHT USE TO DESCRIBE THE WAY IN WHICH RAIN FALLS
to fall   to pour down   to pelt down   to patter

rain *verb*
It's still raining.
▶ to drizzle (*to rain lightly*)   to spit (*to rain lightly*)   to pour

raise *verb*
1 *A crane raised the car out of the ditch.*
▶ to lift   to hoist
2 *Our school is trying to raise money for charity.*
▶ to make   to get   to collect

rare *adjective*
Pandas are very rare animals.
▶ uncommon   unusual   scarce
←→ An opposite is **common**.

rather *adverb*
The water's rather cold.
▶ quite   fairly   pretty

ration *noun*
Each person was given a daily ration of food.
▶ a share   an allowance   a quota   a measure

ray *noun*
A ray of light shone through the crack in the door.
▶ a beam   a shaft

reach *verb*
1 I reached out my hand to pick up the packet.
▶ to stretch
2 Can you reach the biscuit tin?
▶ to touch   to grasp   to get hold of
3 It was dark when we reached London.
▶ to get to It was dark when we got to London.
  to arrive at/in It was dark when we arrived in London.

read *verb*
1 I read the magazine quickly while I was waiting.
▶ to look at   to flick through   to browse through
2 The police have spent hours reading all the important documents.
▶ to read through   to study   to pore over

ready *adjective*
1 Are you ready to leave?
▶ prepared   all set   waiting
2 Your goods are now ready for you to collect.
▶ available
3 Is lunch ready?
▶ prepared   cooked

a
b
c
d
e
f
g
h
i
j
k
l
m
n
o
p
q
r
s
t
u
v
w
x
y
z

real *adjective*

1 *Is that a real diamond?*
   ▶ genuine authentic
   ←→ An opposite is **artificial**.

2 *I've never seen a real elephant before.*
   ▶ real live

3 *Is Tiny your real name?*
   ▶ actual proper
   ←→ An opposite is **false**.

4 *She had never felt real sadness before.*
   ▶ true sincere

realistic *adjective*
We used fake blood, but it looked quite realistic.
   ▶ lifelike natural authentic
   ←→ An opposite is **unrealistic**.

realize *verb*

1 *I suddenly realized that everyone was looking at me.*
   ▶ to become aware to notice to see

2 *I suddenly realized that he had been lying to me.*
   ▶ to understand to know to see to comprehend

really *adverb*

1 *The water's really cold!*
   ▶ very extremely

2 *Are you really sorry?*
   ▶ truly honestly genuinely

3 *Is your dad really a spy?*
   ▶ actually

rear *noun*
He crashed into the rear of a bus.
   ▶ the back the end
   ←→ An opposite is **front**.

rear *verb*
The male lions play no part in rearing the cubs.
▶ to look after   to care for   to bring up

reason *noun*
1 *There must be a reason why this plant has died.*
▶ a cause   an explanation
2 *What was your reason for telling us these lies?*
▶ a motive

reasonable *adjective*
1 *It is reasonable to expect you to tidy your own bedroom.*
▶ fair   right
← → An opposite is **unreasonable**.
2 *Let's try and discuss this in a reasonable way.*
▶ sensible   rational   mature
← → An opposite is **irrational**.
3 *You can earn a reasonable amount of money.*
▶ fair   quite good   respectable

rebel *verb*
1 *The soldiers rebelled.*
▶ to revolt   to rise up   to mutiny   to disobey orders
2 *The sailors on the ship rebelled.*
▶ to mutiny

receive *verb*
1 *I received some lovely presents.*
▶ to get
to be given *I was given some lovely presents.*
2 *How much money do you receive each week for doing the paper round?*
▶ to get   to earn
← → An opposite is **give**.

recent *adjective*
Her recent film is not as good as the others.
▶ new   latest   current   up-to-date

reckon *verb*

I reckon our side will win.
> to think   to believe   to feel sure

recognize *verb*

Would you recognize that man if you saw him again?
> to remember   to know   to identify

recommend *verb*

1 *A lot of people have recommended this book to me.*
> to suggest
> to speak highly of *A lot of people have spoken highly of this book.*

2 *I recommend that you should see a doctor.*
> to suggest   to advise *I advise you to see a doctor.*

record *noun*

We kept a record of the birds we saw on holiday.
> an account   a diary   a list   a journal   a log

recover *verb*

Have you recovered from your illness?
> to get better   to get well   to recuperate

red *adjective*

1 *She was wearing a red dress.*
> crimson   scarlet   maroon

2 *Her cheeks were red.*
> rosy   glowing   flushed

reduce *verb*

1 *She reduced speed when she saw the police car.*
> to decrease

2 *We want to reduce the amount of litter in the playground.*
> to lessen   to cut down

3 *The shop has reduced all its prices.*
> to lower   to cut   to slash
> to halve *(to reduce by half)*

←→ An opposite is **increase**.

a b c d e f g h i j k l m n o p q **r** s t u v w x y z

200

refer to *verb*
He referred to the story he had read.
▶ to mention   to comment on   to talk about

refreshed *adjective*
I felt refreshed after my rest.
▶ invigorated   restored   revived

refreshing *adjective*
1 *I had a lovely refreshing shower.*
▶ invigorating
2 *I need a refreshing drink.*
▶ cooling   thirst-quenching

refuse *verb*
I offered to take him to the party, but he refused.
▶ to say no *He said no.*
to decline *He declined.*
to be unwilling *He was unwilling.*
←→ An opposite is **accept**.

region *noun*
These animals only live in hot regions.
▶ an area   a place   a zone

regret *verb*
I was very rude to my parents, and I regret it now.
▶ to be sorry for *I am sorry for it now.*
to be ashamed of *I am ashamed of it now.*
to repent *I repent of it now.*

regular *adjective*
1 *You should take regular exercise.*
▶ frequent   daily   weekly
2 *The postman was on his regular delivery round.*
▶ normal   usual   customary
3 *The drummer kept a regular rhythm.*
▶ even   steady
←→ An opposite is **irregular**.

rehearse *verb*

1 *We rehearsed for the concert all afternoon.*
▶ **to practise   to prepare**

2 *I think you should rehearse your speech.*
▶ **to go through   to run through**

reject *verb*
My friends rejected my suggestion.
▶ **to say no to** *They said no to my suggestion.*
to turn down *They turned down my suggestion.*
to refuse to accept *They refused to accept my suggestion.*
◀ ▶ An opposite is **accept**.

relation *noun*
She is a relation of mine.
▶ **a relative**

relax *verb*

1 *I like to relax after school.*
▶ **to rest   to unwind   to take it easy**

2 *Relax, there's nothing to worry about.*
▶ **to calm down   to not panic** *Don't panic!*

release *verb*
They released the animals from the cage.
▶ **to free   to liberate**
to set free *They set the animals free.*
to turn loose *They turned the animals loose.*
to let out *They let the animals out.*

reliable *adjective*
I'm surprised that Joshua is late, he's usually so reliable.
▶ **dependable   responsible   trustworthy**
◀ ▶ An opposite is **unreliable**.

relieved *adjective*
I was very relieved when I heard that no one was hurt.
▶ **happy   glad   thankful**

religion *noun*
Different people follow different religions.
▶ a belief   a faith   a creed

●●● SOME DIFFERENT RELIGIONS
Buddhism	Christianity	Hinduism
Islam	Judaism	Sikhism

religious *adjective*
They got married in a special religious ceremony.
▶ holy   sacred

reluctant *adjective*
I was reluctant to walk home because it was raining.
▶ unwilling   unhappy   not keen   hesitant
←→ An opposite is **keen**.

rely on *verb*
1 the young chicks rely on their mother for food.
▶ to depend on   to need
2 We know we can always rely on you to help us.
▶ to trust   to count on

remain *verb*
Please remain in your seats.
▶ to stay   to wait

remains *noun*
1 We visited the remains of a Roman castle.
▶ ruins   remnants
2 We gave the remains of the food to the dog.
▶ the leftovers   the rest

remark *verb*
I remarked that it was a nice day.
▶ to comment   to mention   to observe   to point out

remarkable *adjective*
This was a remarkable achievement.
▶ extraordinary   amazing   astonishing   incredible
←→ An opposite is **ordinary**.

remember *verb*

1 *I can't remember his name.*
▶ to recall   to recollect

> 66 99 ANOTHER WAY OF SAYING *I can't remember his name.*
>   *I've forgotten his name.*

2 *I'm going to give you my phone number, and you must remember it.*
▶ to learn   to memorize   to make a mental note of
← → An opposite is **forget**.

remind *verb*

Seeing her with her swimming kit reminded me that I needed mine.
▶ to jog someone's memory *Seeing her with her swimming kit jogged my memory.*

remove *verb*

1 *Please remove this rubbish.*
▶ to take away   to carry away   to get rid of   to move

2 *He opened the drawer and removed some of the papers.*
▶ to take out   to lift out   to get out

3 *The dentist removed two of my teeth.*
▶ to extract   to take out

4 *He carefully removed the front of the TV set.*
▶ to take off   to detach

5 *She carefully removed the stamp from the envelope.*
▶ to tear off   to cut off   to peel off

6 *Someone had removed the door handle.*
▶ to take off   to break off   to snap off

7 *He walked into the house and removed his shoes.*
▶ to take off   to kick off

8 *We scrubbed the walls to remove the dirt.*
▶ to get off   to wipe off   to scrape off   to scratch off   to rub off

9 *I removed her name from the list.*
▶ to cross out   to rub out   to erase   to delete

10 *I accidentally removed some files from my computer.*
▶ to delete   to wipe out

11 *The police removed him from the building.*
▶ to evict   to throw out

repair *verb*

She managed to repair the TV.
► **to mend   to fix   to put right** *She managed to put it right.*

repeat *verb*

Could you repeat that, please?
► **to say again** *Could you say that again, please?*
reiterate *Mum reiterated that we must be home by seven o'clock.*

reply *noun*

I called her name, but there was no reply.
► **an answer   a response**

reply *verb*

I asked him another question, but he didn't reply.
► **to answer   to respond**

report *noun*

1 *We had to write a report of what had happened.*
► **an account   a description**
2 *There was a report about our school in the local newspaper.*
► **an article   a story**

rescue *verb*

1 *Robin Hood rescued the prisoners from the Sheriff's castle.*
► **to free   to release   to liberate**
to set free *He set the prisoners free.*
2 *The firemen managed to rescue the children from the fire.*
► **to save**

reserve *noun*

Each team is allowed three reserves.
► **a substitute**

reserve *verb*

We reserved our seats on the train.
► **to book**

resign *verb*

Our teacher resigned at the end of last term.
► **to leave   to quit**

respect

respect *verb*

I respect my grandparents.
> to look up to   to admire   to think highly of

respect *noun*

You should always treat other people with respect.
> consideration   thoughtfulness   courtesy   politeness

responsible *adjective*

1 *You are responsible for feeding the fish.*
> in charge of *You are in charge of feeding the fish.*

2 *Who is responsible for breaking this window?*
> to blame for *Who is to blame for breaking this window?*
guilty of *Who is guilty of breaking this window?*

3 *We need a responsible person to look after the money.*
> sensible   reliable   trustworthy
←→ An opposite is **irresponsible**.

rest *noun*

1 *We stopped for a quick rest.*
> a break   a pause   a sit-down   a lie-down   a breather

2 *The doctor says that she needs plenty of rest.*
> sleep   relaxation

3 *If you have finished, the dog will eat the rest.*
> the remainder

rest *verb*

We'll rest for half an hour before we continue.
> to relax   to take it easy   to sit down   to lie down   to sleep
to have a nap

result *noun*

1 *As a result of our good behaviour we got extra playtime.*
> a consequence   an outcome

2 *I didn't see the match, but I know the result.*
> a score

retreat *verb*

The soldiers retreated towards the fort.
> to go back   to move back   to withdraw   to flee

a
b
c
d
e
f
g
h
i
j
k
l
m
n
o
p
q
r
s
t
u
v
w
x
y
z

return *verb*
1 *We decided to return to the cave.*
▶ **to go back**
2 *He left, and we didn't know if he would ever return.*
▶ **to come back   to reappear**

reveal *verb*
1 *He opened the door and revealed a secret room.*
▶ **to expose   to show**
2 *She drew back the curtain and revealed a statue of a man.*
▶ **to uncover   to unveil**
3 *Don't ever reveal our secret!*
▶ **to tell   to disclose**
to let out *Don't ever let this secret out.*
to make known *Don't ever make this secret known.*

revenge *noun*
He wanted revenge for the death of his father.
▶ **vengeance   retribution**

reverse *verb*
She reversed the car into the drive.
▶ **to back**

review *noun*
I wrote a review of the book.
▶ **an evaluation   a judgement**

revolting *adjective*
1 *The food was revolting.*
▶ **horrible   disgusting   tasteless   inedible**
2 *What a revolting dress!*
▶ **horrible   vile   hideous   repulsive**
◀ ▶ An opposite is **pleasant**.

rich *adjective*
She dreamed of being rich and famous.
▶ **wealthy   well-off   prosperous**
◀ ▶ An opposite is **poor**.

get rid of *verb*

1 *I'm going to get rid of all these old clothes.*
> ► **to throw away   to throw out   to dispose of**

2 *We must get rid of the evidence.*
> ► **to destroy   to remove**

ridiculous *adjective*

That's a ridiculous thing to say!
> ► **silly   absurd   foolish   stupid   ludicrous   preposterous
> crazy**

← → An opposite is **sensible**.

right *adjective*

1 *That is the right answer.*
> ► **correct**

2 *Is that the right time?*
> ► **exact   precise**

3 *I haven't got the right books.*
> ► **appropriate   suitable   proper**

4 *It's right to own up when you've been naughty.*
> ► **honest   fair   good   sensible   honourable**

← → An opposite is **wrong**.

ring *noun*

We all stood in a ring.
> ► **a circle**

ring *verb*

1 *The doorbell rang.*
> ► **to sound**

2 *We could hear the church bells ringing.*
> ► **to chime   to peal**

3 *The bells round the horse's neck rang as it trotted along.*
> ► **to tinkle   to jingle   to jangle**

4 *I'll ring you later.*
> ► **to call   to phone   to telephone**

riot *noun*

There was a riot in the street.
> ► **a disturbance   a commotion**

rip verb

I ripped my jeans.
> ▶ to tear to split

rise verb

1 I watched the balloon rise into the sky.
> ▶ to climb to ascend to go up
> ← → An opposite is **descend**.

2 The sun was rising when we got up.
> ▶ to come up
> ← → An opposite is **set**.

3 Bus fares are going to rise next week.
> ▶ to increase to go up
> ← → An opposite is **fall**.

risk noun

There is a risk that you might fall.
> ▶ a danger a chance a possibility

rival noun

On Saturday we're playing against our old rivals.
> ▶ an opponent an adversary an enemy

river noun

○ Focus on **river**

> We walked along next to the river.
> ▶ a stream (a small river)
> a brook (a small stream)
> a canal (a man-made river)

SOME WORDS YOU MIGHT USE TO DESCRIBE A RIVER

wide	broad	great
mighty	small	narrow
deep	shallow	fast-moving
slow-moving	winding	meandering

SOME WORDS YOU MIGHT USE TO DESCRIBE THE WAY IN
WHICH A RIVER MOVES ALONG

to flow	to wind	to run
to rush		

road *noun*

1 *We live in a road just off the High Street.*
   ▶ a street   an avenue   a close
2 *There is a narrow road between the two farms.*
   ▶ a track   a path   a lane   an alley
3 *There were a lot of cars on the road between Birmingham and London.*
   ▶ a main road   a motorway

roar *verb*
The crowd roared.
   ▶ to bellow   to shout   to cry   to yell

robber *noun*
The robbers managed to escape.
   ▶ a burglar   a thief   a crook   a pickpocket   a shoplifter

rock *noun*
He picked up a rock and hurled it into the sea.
   ▶ a stone
      a boulder (*a very big rock*)

rock *verb*

1 *The little boat rocked gently in the breeze.*
   ▶ to sway   to swing
2 *The ship rocked violently in the storm.*
   ▶ to roll   to toss   to pitch

roll *verb*
The logs rolled down the hill.
   ▶ to spin   to tumble   to slide

room *noun*
Is there enough room for me to sit down?
   ▶ space

rope *noun*
The boat was tied up with a strong rope.
   ▶ a cable   a line   a cord

rotten *adjective*

1 *The wood was old and rotten.*
- ▶ decayed decomposed
- ←→ An opposite is **sound**.

2 *We couldn't eat the meat because it was rotten.*
- ▶ old mouldy bad off
- ←→ An opposite is **fresh**.

3 *That was a rotten thing to do!*
- ▶ nasty unkind mean horrible
- ←→ An opposite is **good**.

rough *adjective*

1 *We jolted along the rough road.*
- ▶ bumpy uneven stony rocky
- ←→ An opposite is **even**.

2 *Sandpaper feels rough.*
- ▶ coarse scratchy prickly
- ←→ An opposite is **smooth**.

3 *He spoke in a rough voice.*
- ▶ gruff husky hoarse
- ←→ An opposite is **soft**.

4 *The sea was very rough.*
- ▶ stormy choppy
- ←→ An opposite is **calm**.

5 *I don't like rough games.*
- ▶ boisterous rowdy
- ←→ An opposite is **gentle**.

6 *Don't be so rough with your little brother.*
- ▶ violent aggressive
- ←→ An opposite is **gentle**.

7 *At a rough guess, I would say there were fifty people there.*
- ▶ approximate estimated
- ←→ An opposite is **exact**.

round *adjective*

He was wearing a round badge.
- ▶ circular

a
b
c
d
e
f
g
h
i
j
k
l
m
n
o
p
q
r
s
t
u
v
w
x
y
z

row noun (rhymes with **cow**)
1 *I had a row with my sister.*
▶ **an argument a quarrel a disagreement a fight
a squabble**
2 *What's that terrible row?*
▶ **noise din racket rumpus uproar**

row noun (rhymes with **toe**)
We stood in a straight row.
▶ **a line a queue**

rub verb
1 *He rubbed the paint to see if it would come off.*
▶ **to scratch to scrape**
2 *He rubbed the old coin to make it shine.*
▶ **to clean to polish**

rub out verb
She rubbed out what she had just written.
▶ **to erase to remove to delete**

rubbish noun
1 *The rubbish is collected from people's homes once a week.*
▶ **refuse waste garbage trash** (American)
2 *There was rubbish all over the playground.*
▶ **litter**
3 *The garage is full of old rubbish.*
▶ **junk**
4 *You're talking rubbish!*
▶ **nonsense balderdash drivel**

rude adjective
1 *Don't be rude to your teacher.*
▶ **cheeky impertinent impudent insolent disrespectful**
2 *It was very rude to walk away while I was talking to you.*
▶ **bad-mannered impolite**
3 *They got told off for telling rude jokes.*
▶ **indecent dirty vulgar**
← → An opposite is **polite**.

ruin *verb*

1 *The storm ruined the farmers' crops.*
   ▶ to spoil   to damage   to destroy   to wreck
2 *The bad weather ruined our holiday.*
   ▶ to spoil   to mess up

rule *noun*

It is a school rule that all children must wear school uniform.
   ▶ a regulation   a law

rule *verb*

In the old days, the king used to rule the country.
   ▶ to govern   to control   to run

ruler *noun*

Who is the ruler of this country?
   ▶ a king   a queen   a monarch (*a king or queen*)
   a sovereign (*a king or queen*)   an emperor   an empress
   a president

run *verb*

!!! **run** *is a word that is often overused.*

1 *Do you enjoy running?*
   ▶ to jog   to sprint   to race
2 *We ran across the field.*
   ▶ to race   to tear   to charge   to career   to fly
3 *You'll have to run if you want to catch the bus.*
   ▶ to rush   to dash   to hurry
4 *The dog ran off.*
   ▶ to bound   to scamper
5 *We could see the horses running across the field.*
   ▶ to trot   to canter   to gallop
6 *The little mouse ran into its hole.*
   ▶ to scurry   to scuttle   to scamper
7 *He runs a drama club after school.*
   ▶ to be in charge of   to manage

a b c d e f g h i j k l m n o p q **r** s t u v w x y z

a
b
c
d
e
f
g
h
i
j
k
l
m
n
o
p
q
r
s
t
u
v
w
x
y
z

run away *verb*
I chased them but they ran away.
▶ to escape   to get away   to flee

runny *adjective*
The jelly hasn't set yet—it's still runny.
▶ watery   sloppy   liquid

rush *verb*
I rushed to the bus stop.
▶ to dash   to hurry   to run   to race

Ss

sacred *adjective*
The Bible and the Koran are sacred books.
▶ holy religious

sad *adjective*
1 *The little boy looked very sad.*
▶ unhappy upset miserable fed up dejected despondent depressed gloomy glum down in the dumps heartbroken
2 *I was very sad when we lost in the final.*
▶ upset disappointed
3 *This is very sad news.*
▶ upsetting tragic depressing distressing disappointing
← → An opposite is **happy**.

safe *adjective*
1 *Once we reached the boat I knew that we were safe.*
▶ secure out of danger out of harm's way
← → An opposite is **in danger**.
2 *We were glad to get home safe.*
▶ safe and sound unharmed in one piece
← → An opposite is **hurt**.
3 *We stayed in the shed where we would be safe from the storm.*
▶ sheltered protected
← → An opposite is **in danger**.
4 *Castles were very safe places.*
▶ secure well-protected well-defended impregnable
← → An opposite is **dangerous**.
5 *Is this ladder safe?*
▶ firm secure strong enough
← → An opposite is **dangerous**.
6 *Tigers are wild animals and are never completely safe.*
▶ harmless tame
← → An opposite is **dangerous**.

sail *verb*

1 *We're sailing to France tomorrow.*
▶ to set sail   to go by ship
2 *We watched the yachts sailing on the lake.*
▶ to float   to glide   to drift   to bob
3 *The ship sailed out of the harbour.*
▶ to steam   to chug

sake *noun*
I did this for your sake.
▶ benefit

same *adjective*
The houses look the same.
▶ identical   similar   alike
←→ An opposite is **different**.

satisfactory *adjective*
Your work is satisfactory, but I think you could do better.
▶ all right   OK   acceptable   fair   adequate
←→ An opposite is **unsatisfactory**.

satisfied *adjective*
The teacher was satisfied with the children's behaviour.
▶ pleased   happy
←→ An opposite is **dissatisfied**.

save *verb*

1 *A fireman climbed into the burning building to save her.*
▶ to rescue   to free   to liberate   to release
2 *I saved some sweets for later.*
▶ to keep   to put aside *I put some sweets aside for later.*

say verb

> !!! **say** is a word that is often overused.

1 *He said that he might be late.*
> ► to mention   to remark   to explain   to hint

2 *'Where's the key?' 'I don't know,' she said.*
> ► to answer   to reply   to respond

3 *'She's very tall,' he said.*
> ► to comment   to observe   to remark   to point out

4 *'We're leaving tomorrow,' she said.*
> ► to announce   to declare

5 *'Why don't you phone him?' she said.*
> ► to suggest

6 *'I don't care!' she said.*
> ► to shout   to cry   to yell   to scream   to shriek

7 *'It must be here somewhere,' he said quietly to himself.*
> ► to mutter   to mumble   to murmur   to whisper

8 *'You're late again!' he said angrily.*
> ► to snap   to growl   to snarl

9 *'Oh dear,' she said.*
> ► to sigh

10 *'A b-b-bomb?' he said.*
> ► to stutter   to stammer   to splutter

11 *'I suppose you think you're clever,' she said.*
> ► to laugh   to sneer   to scoff   to jeer

saying noun
Do you know that saying about too many cooks?
> ► a proverb   an expression   a phrase

scare verb
1 *The sudden noise scared me.*
> ► to frighten   to startle
> to make someone jump *The noise made me jump.*
> to give someone a fright *The noise gave me a fright.*

2 *The thought of changing schools really scares me.*
> ► to frighten   to terrify

scared adjective
Are you scared of mice?
> ► frightened   afraid   terrified   petrified (very scared indeed)

a
b
c
d
e
f
g
h
i
j
k
l
m
n
o
p
q
r
s
t
u
v
w
x
y
z

scary *adjective*
It was quite scary being in the old house alone.
▶ **eerie frightening terrifying**

scold *verb*
The teacher scolded us for being late.
▶ **to tell off** *The teacher told us off.*
to reprimand

scramble *verb*
We scrambled over the rocks.
▶ **to climb to clamber to crawl**

scrape *verb*
We scraped the mud off our shoes.
▶ **to rub to clean to scrub**

scratch *verb*
1 *Mind you don't scratch the paint on the car.*
▶ **to damage to scrape to mark**
2 *His head was itching so he scratched it.*
▶ **to rub**

scream *verb*
1 *Everyone screamed when the ride went faster and faster.*
▶ **to cry out to shriek to squeal**
2 *'Go away!' she screamed.*
▶ **to cry to shout to call to yell to shriek**

sea *noun*
1 *We are trying to learn more about creatures that live in the sea.*
▶ **the ocean the deep**
2 *They sailed across the sea.*
▶ **the ocean the water the waves**

seal *verb*
Remember to seal the envelope.
▶ **to stick down to close**

a
b
c
d
e
f
g
h
i
j
k
l
m
n
o
p
q
r
s
t
u
v
w
x
y
z

search *verb*
I was searching for my watch.
▶ to look for   to hunt for   to try to find

seaside *noun*
We spent the day at the seaside.
▶ the beach   the coast

seat *noun*
I sat down on a seat by the door.
▶ a chair

> ••• SOME TYPES OF SEAT
>
> | | |
> |---|---|
> | an armchair | a bench |
> | a highchair (*a child's seat*) | |
> | a rocking chair | a settee |
> | a sofa | a stool |

secret *adjective*
1 *She wrote everything down in her secret diary.*
▶ personal   private
2 *There is a secret passage under the castle.*
▶ hidden   concealed

see *verb*
1 *I saw a horse in the field.*
▶ to notice   to observe   to spot   to spy
2 *Out of the corner of my eye I saw a boy.*
▶ to catch sight of   to glimpse   to catch a glimpse of
3 *I could just see the hills in the distance.*
▶ to make out
4 *We saw a very good film yesterday.*
▶ to watch
5 *No one saw the accident.*
▶ to witness
6 *I'm going to see my grandma tomorrow.*
▶ to visit   to pay a visit to   to call on
7 *I see what you mean.*
▶ to understand   to know

seem *verb*
Everyone seems very happy today.
▶ **to appear   to look   to sound**

seize *verb*
1 I seized the end of the rope.
▶ **to grab   to take hold of**
2 The thief seized my bag and ran off.
▶ **to grab   to snatch**
3 The police seized the two men.
▶ **to arrest   to catch   to capture**

select *verb*
She opened the box and selected a chocolate.
▶ **to choose   to pick**

selfish *adjective*
You shouldn't be so selfish.
▶ **mean   self-centred   thoughtless**
← → An opposite is **unselfish**.

sell *verb*
1 This shop sells exotic tropical fish.
▶ **to deal in   to stock**
2 I sold my old bike to one of my friends.
▶ **to flog** (informal)

> ❝❞ ANOTHER WAY OF SAYING *I sold my old bike to one of my friends.*
> *One of my friends bought my old bike from me.*

send *verb*
1 I sent a birthday card to my cousin.
▶ **to post**
2 The teacher sent her out of the room.
▶ **to order**

a
b
c
d
e
f
g
h
i
j
k
l
m
n
o
p
q
r
s
t
u
v
w
x
y
z

sense *noun*
> *That child has got no sense!*
> ▶ **common sense intelligence brains**

sensible *adjective*
> **1** *She is usually a very sensible girl.*
> ▶ **careful thoughtful level-headed responsible mature
> wise**
> **2** *I think that would be the sensible thing to do.*
> ▶ **logical prudent**
> ← → An opposite is **stupid**.

sensitive *adjective*
> **1** *Tom is a very sensitive boy.*
> ▶ **easily hurt touchy**
> ← → An opposite is **insensitive**.
> **2** *You shouldn't use this suncream if you have sensitive skin.*
> ▶ **delicate**

separate *adjective*
> **1** *We need to keep the two piles separate.*
> ▶ **apart**
> **2** *The two brothers sleep in separate bedrooms.*
> ▶ **different**
> ← → An opposite is **together**.

separate *verb*
> **1** *It's a good idea to separate the foreign stamps from the British ones.*
> ▶ **to divide to split to remove**
> **2** *The two girls wouldn't stop talking, so the teacher separated them.*
> ▶ **to move**
> **to split up** *The teacher split them up.*
> **to break up** *The teacher broke them up.*

series *noun*
> *There has been a series of accidents in the playground.*
> ▶ **a succession a string**

a
b
c
d
e
f
g
h
i
j
k
l
m
n
o
p
q
r
s
t
u
v
w
x
y
z

serious *adjective*

1 *The old man was looking very serious.*
▶ sad solemn grave thoughtful
←→ An opposite is **cheerful**.

2 *Are you serious about wanting to help?*
▶ sincere genuine
←→ An opposite is **insincere**.

3 *This is a very serious problem.*
▶ important significant
←→ An opposite is **unimportant**.

4 *Several people were hurt in the serious accident.*
▶ bad terrible awful dreadful
←→ An opposite is **minor**.

5 *She has a very serious illness.*
▶ bad dangerous life-threatening
←→ An opposite is **minor**.

set *noun*
I need to get one more card, then I'll have the whole set.
▶ a collection a series

set *verb*

1 *The teacher forgot to set us any homework.*
▶ to give

2 *Please will you set the table for tea?*
▶ to lay to prepare

3 *We'll camp for the night when the sun sets.*
▶ to go down

4 *Has the glue set yet?*
▶ to harden to solidify

set off *verb*
We'll set off early tomorrow morning.
▶ to leave to depart to set out

settle down *verb*
She settled down to watch a film.
▶ to sit down to sit back
to make yourself comfortable *She made herself comfortable.*

sew *verb*
Sew the two pieces together.
▶ to stitch   to tack (*to sew loosely*)

shade *noun*
Stay in the shade if it's very hot.
▶ the shadow

shadow *noun*
We sat in the shadow of a big tree.
▶ the shade

shady *adjective*
We found a shady place to eat our lunch.
▶ cool   shaded
←→ An opposite is **sunny**.

shake *verb*
1 I picked up the money box and shook it.
▶ to rattle
2 The whole house seemed to shake.
▶ to move to rock to sway to wobble to vibrate to shudder
3 The old truck shook as it drove along the bumpy lane.
▶ to judder to jolt to rattle
4 I was shaking with fear.
▶ to tremble to quake to quiver to shiver to shudder

shallow *adjective*
The water's quite shallow here.
▶ not very deep
←→ An opposite is **deep**.

shame *noun*
1 His face was red with shame.
▶ embarrassment   guilt   humiliation   disgrace
2 It's a shame you can't come to the party.
▶ a pity

> **❝ ❞** ANOTHER WAY OF SAYING *It's a shame you can't come to the party.*
> *It's unfortunate that you can't come to the party.*

shape *noun*

1 *In the darkness I could just see the shape of a building.*
 ▶ the outline
2 *He's a powerful magician who can take on any shape he chooses.*
 ▶ a form

● ● ● SOME DIFFERENT SHAPES

a circle	an oval	a pentagon
a hexagon	a heptagon	an octagon
a polygon	a square	a rectangle
a quadrilateral	a triangle	

SOME 3D SHAPES

a sphere	a prism	a cube
a cuboid	a cone	

---

share *noun*

1 *Don't worry, you will get your share of the money.*
 ▶ a part
2 *Mum made sure that everyone had a fair share of the cake.*
 ▶ a portion

share *verb*

We shared the food between us.
 ▶ to divide   to split

sharp *adjective*

1 *Be careful, that knife is sharp.*
 ▶ razor-sharp
 ← → An opposite is **blunt**.
2 *It hurt our feet walking over the sharp rocks.*
 ▶ pointed   jagged
 ← → An opposite is **smooth**.
3 *A hedgehog's body is covered in sharp spines.*
 ▶ prickly   spiky
 ← → An opposite is **smooth**.
4 *There was a sharp bend in the road.*
 ▶ sudden   tight
 ← → An opposite is **gradual**.
5 *He's a very sharp boy.*
 ▶ clever   intelligent   bright   brainy   quick   smart
 ← → An opposite is **stupid**.

a b c d e f g h i j k l m n o p q r s t u v w x y z

shed *noun*

There's a shed at the bottom of the garden.
▶ a hut   an outhouse   a shack

shed *verb*

1 Some trees shed their leaves in the winter.
▶ to drop   to lose

2 Snakes shed their old skin each year.
▶ to cast off

3 A lorry shed its load on the motorway.
▶ to drop   to spill

sheet *noun*

Have you got a spare sheet of paper?
▶ a piece   a page

shelter *noun*

The trees gave us some shelter from the rain.
▶ protection   refuge   cover

shelter *verb*

1 We sheltered from the storm in an old barn.
▶ to hide   to stay safe

2 The hedge sheltered us from the wind.
▶ to protect   to shield

shine *verb*

1 The sun shone all day.
▶ to be out   The sun was out all day.
   to blaze down   to beat down

2 I saw a light shining in the distance.
▶ to glow   to glimmer   to gleam   to flash   to flicker

3 The stars shone in the night sky.
▶ to twinkle   to sparkle

4 The water of the lake shone in the moonlight.
▶ to shimmer   to glisten   to sparkle

5 The diamonds shone in the sunlight.
▶ to sparkle   to glint   to glitter

a
b
c
d
e
f
g
h
i
j
k
l
m
n
o
p
q
r
s
t
u
v
w
x
y
z

shiny *adjective*

1 *We found a shiny new coin.*
  ▶ bright gleaming
2 *He was wearing shiny shoes.*
  ▶ polished
3 *We printed our designs on shiny paper.*
  ▶ glossy
◀▶ An opposite is **dull**.

shiver *verb*

1 *I was shivering with cold.*
  ▶ to shake
2 *She was shivering with fear.*
  ▶ to shake to tremble to quake to quiver to shudder

shock *verb*

1 *The explosion shocked everyone.*
  ▶ to frighten to startle to alarm to shake
2 *News of the terrible accident shocked us all.*
  ▶ to upset to distress
3 *The swearing in the film shocked us.*
  ▶ to offend to disgust to horrify

shocked *adjective*

1 *I felt quite shocked when I realized I had won.*
  ▶ surprised astonished astounded staggered
2 *Everyone was shocked by the terrible accident.*
  ▶ upset distressed traumatized
3 *I was shocked when I heard the children swearing.*
  ▶ disgusted appalled horrified

shoe *noun*

SOME TYPES OF SHOE			
boots	plimsolls	pumps	sandals
slippers	trainers	wellingtons	

shoot *verb*

Try to shoot straight.
  ▶ to fire to aim

shop *noun*

You can buy sweets in the shop on the corner.
▶ a store

• • • SOME BIG SHOPS

a department store a hypermarket a supermarket

SOME OTHER TYPES OF SHOP

a baker	a book shop	a boutique
a butcher	a chemist	a clothes shop
a delicatessen	a fishmonger	a florist
a gift shop	a grocer	an ironmonger
a jeweller	a music shop	a newsagent
a post office	a shoe shop	a toy shop

---

short *adjective*

1 *I'm quite short for my age.*
▶ small little
← → An opposite is **tall**.

2 *It was a strange animal, with a long body and short legs.*
▶ stumpy stubby
← → An opposite is **long**.

3 *We're only staying for a short time.*
▶ brief
← → An opposite is **long**.

4 *It was just a short visit.*
▶ brief fleeting quick

shout *verb*

1 *The man shouted at me to go away.*
▶ to scream to yell to shriek to bawl to bellow

2 *'Help!' she shouted.*
▶ to cry to call to scream to yell to shriek

3 *'Hooray!' they shouted.*
▶ to cheer

4 *'You're useless!' they shouted.*
▶ to jeer
← → An opposite is **whisper**.

a
b
c
d
e
f
g
h
i
j
k
l
m
n
o
p
q
r

s

t
u
v
w
x
y
z

show *noun*

We're putting on a school show at the end of term.
▶ **a performance   a production   a play   a concert**

show *verb*

1 *Shall I show you my new bike?*
▶ **to let someone see** *I'll let you see my new bike.*

2 *He showed me the place where the accident happened.*
▶ **to point to**
to indicate *He indicated the place where the accident*

happened.

3 *We showed our work to the visitors.*
▶ **to display   to exhibit**

4 *She showed me how to use the computer.*
▶ **to tell   to teach**
to explain *She explained to me how to use the computer.*

5 *They're showing all the James Bond films on TV at the moment.*
▶ **to put on**

show off *verb*

Stop showing off!
▶ **to boast   to brag   to gloat**

shrivel *verb*

The plants shrivelled in the heat.
▶ **to dry up   to wither**

shut *verb*

She went out of the room and shut the door.
▶ **to close   to fasten   to pull shut   to push shut   to lock**
to bolt
to slam *(to shut noisily)*
to bang *(to shut noisily)*
←→ An opposite is **open**.

shut up *verb*

The boy told us to shut up.
▶ to be quiet   to keep quiet   to be silent

shy *adjective*

He was too shy to say that he knew the answer.
▶ nervous   timid   bashful   modest

sick *adjective*

1 *I stayed off school because I was sick.*
▶ ill   unwell   poorly

2 *After eating all that chocolate I felt really sick.*
▶ queasy

3 *I was sick twice in the night.*
▶ ill

> ❝ ❞ OTHER WAYS OF SAYING *I was sick.*
> *I vomited.*
> *I threw up.*

side *noun*

1 *Some people were standing at one side of the field.*
▶ an edge

2 *We waited at the side of the road.*
▶ the edge   the verge

sight *noun*

She is quite old and doesn't have very good sight.
▶ eyesight   vision

sign *noun*

1 *The sign for a dollar is $.*
▶ a symbol   a logo

2 *There was a sign telling people to keep off the grass.*
▶ a notice   a signpost

3 *I'll give you a sign when I'm ready for you to start.*
▶ a signal   a gesture

a b c d e f g h i j k l m n o p q r s t u v w x y z

signal noun
Don't move until I give the signal.
> ▸ a sign   a gesture

silent adjective
1 *The hall was empty and silent.*
> ▸ quiet   peaceful   noiseless
> ←→ An opposite is **noisy**.

2 *The teacher told us to be silent.*
> ▸ quiet
> ←→ An opposite is **talkative**.

3 *I asked him some questions, but he remained silent.*
> ▸ tight-lipped

silly adjective
1 *It's silly to go out in the rain.*
> ▸ daft   foolish   stupid   unwise

2 *Please stop this silly behaviour.*
> ▸ childish   immature

3 *Why are you wearing such silly clothes?*
> ▸ ridiculous   peculiar   odd   unsuitable

similar adjective
The two girls look quite similar.
> ▸ alike   identical   the same
> ←→ An opposite is **different**.

simple adjective
1 *That's a simple question.*
> ▸ easy   straightforward
> ←→ An opposite is **difficult**.

2 *The explanation is quite simple—he's lying.*
> ▸ clear   obvious
> ←→ An opposite is **complicated**.

3 *We used quite a simple design for our poster.*
> ▸ plain   not fancy
> ←→ An opposite is **elaborate**.

sing *verb*
1 *He was singing quietly to himself.*
▶ **to hum**
2 *The birds were singing in the trees.*
▶ **to chirp to cheep to twitter to warble**

sink *verb*
The ship sank in a storm.
▶ **to go down to founder**
to be submerged *The ship was submerged.*

site *noun*
This would be a very good site for the new school.
▶ **a place a spot a position a location**

situation *noun*
1 *This is a terrible situation.*
▶ **a state of affairs**
2 *I wouldn't like to be in your situation.*
▶ **a position**

size *noun*
What is the size of this room?
▶ **the measurements the dimensions the length the width the breadth the height**

> 6 9 **ANOTHER WAY OF SAYING** *What is the size of the room?*
> *How big is the room?*

skate *verb*
He skated gracefully over the ice.
▶ **to glide to slide to float**

skilful *adjective*
He is a skilful player.
▶ **talented clever competent**

a b c d e f g h i j k l m n o p q r s t u v w x y z

231

a
b
c
d
e
f
g
h
i
j
k
l
m
n
o
p
q
r
s
t
u
v
w
x
y
z

skill *noun*
Everyone admired her skill.
▶ ability   talent   expertise

skin *noun*
1 *Their clothes were made of animal skins.*
▶ a hide   a fur   a pelt
2 *You can eat the skin on some fruits but not others.*
▶ the rind   the peel

skip *verb*
1 *She skipped happily down the road.*
▶ to dance   to prance   to trip   to trot
2 *The lambs were skipping about in the fields.*
▶ to jump   to leap   to frisk   to prance

sledge *noun*
The children were playing on sledges.
▶ a toboggan
a sleigh (*a big sledge that is pulled by animals*)

sleep *verb*
1 *He was sleeping in front of the fire.*
▶ to be asleep   to fall asleep   to doze   to snooze   to slumber
to snore   to have a nap   to nod off
2 *Some animals sleep all winter.*
▶ to hibernate

sleepy *adjective*
I was sleepy so I went to bed.
▶ tired   drowsy   weary
←→ An opposite is **wide awake**.

slide *verb*
1 *The sledge slid across the ice.*
▶ to glide   to skim
2 *The car slid on the icy road.*
▶ to skid   to slip

slight *adjective*
We've got a slight problem.
▶ small   little   minor   unimportant

slim *adjective*
She was tall and slim.
▶ thin   slender

slip *verb*
1 Sam slipped and fell over.
▶ to trip   to stumble
to lose your balance *He lost his balance.*
2 The wheels kept slipping on the wet road.
▶ to slide   to skid

slippery *adjective*
Take care: the floor is slippery.
▶ slithery   slippy   greasy   oily   slimy   icy

slope *noun*
We climbed up the steep slope to the castle.
▶ a hill   a bank   a rise

slope *verb*
1 The beach slopes down to the sea.
▶ to drop   to dip   to fall
2 The field slopes gently upwards towards a wood.
▶ to rise
3 The floor slopes to one side.
▶ to tilt   to slant   to lean

sloppy *adjective*
1 The mixture was still too sloppy.
▶ wet   runny   watery
2 This is a very sloppy piece of work!
▶ careless   messy   untidy   shoddy

slot *noun*
I put a coin in the slot.
▶ a slit   an opening   a groove

a
b
c
d
e
f
g
h
i
j
k
l
m
n
o
p
q
r
s
t
u
v
w
x
y
z

slow *adjective*

1 *Our school bus is always very slow.*
   ▶ slow-moving sluggish
2 *They were walking at a slow pace.*
   ▶ steady leisurely unhurried
3 *He made a slow recovery from his illness.*
   ▶ steady gradual
◀ ➔ An opposite is **quick**.

sly *adjective*
They say the fox is a sly animal.
   ▶ clever crafty cunning wily

smack *verb*
Don't smack your little brother!
   ▶ to slap to hit to spank

small *adjective*

1 *He handed me a small envelope.*
   ▶ little tiny titchy minute
2 *They live in a small flat.*
   ▶ little tiny cramped poky
3 *I'm quite small for my age.*
   ▶ short slight petite
4 *She gave us small helpings.*
   ▶ mean measly stingy
5 *This dress is too small for me.*
   ▶ tight short
6 *It's only a small problem.*
   ▶ little slight minor
◀ ➔ An opposite is **big**.

smart *adjective*

1 *You look very smart in your new clothes.*
   ▶ neat elegant stylish well-dressed chic
   ◀ ➔ An opposite is **scruffy**.
2 *He's a smart boy.*
   ▶ clever intelligent bright
   ◀ ➔ An opposite is **stupid**.

smear *verb*
The baby had smeared jam all over the walls.
▶ to wipe   to rub   to spread   to daub

smell *noun*
1 *There was a lovely smell of flowers.*
   ▶ a scent   a perfume   a fragrance
2 *There were lovely smells of cooking coming from the kitchen.*
   ▶ an aroma
3 *There was a horrible smell of rotting food.*
   ▶ a stink   a stench   an odour

smell *verb*
Your feet smell!
   ▶ to stink   to reek   to pong

smile *verb*
1 *She looked up and smiled at me.*
   ▶ to grin   to beam
2 *Some of the other children smiled unkindly when I got told off.*
   ▶ to smirk

smoke *noun*
The room was full of black smoke.
   ▶ fumes

smooth *adjective*
1 *Roll out the dough on a smooth surface.*
   ▶ level   even   flat
   ←→ An opposite is **uneven**.
2 *I stroked the cat's lovely smooth fur.*
   ▶ soft   silky   velvety   sleek
   ←→ An opposite is **rough**.
3 *We rowed across the smooth surface of the lake.*
   ▶ calm   flat   still
   ←→ An opposite is **rough**.

snatch *verb*
The dog snatched the sandwich out of my hand.
   ▶ to grab   to take   to pull   to seize

a
b
c
d
e
f
g
h
i
j
k
l
m
n
o
p
q
r
s
t
u
v
w
x
y
z

a
b
c
d
e
f
g
h
i
j
k
l
m
n
o
p
q
r
s
t
u
v
w
x
y
z

sneak *verb*
She sneaked out of the room when no one was looking.
▶ to creep to slip to steal

soft *adjective*
1 *Work the clay with your hands until it is nice and soft.*
▶ doughy squashy malleable
←➔ An opposite is **hard**.
2 *The bed was warm and soft.*
▶ springy
←➔ An opposite is **hard**.
3 *The kitten's coat was lovely and soft.*
▶ smooth fluffy furry silky velvety
←➔ An opposite is **rough**.
4 *Our feet sank into the soft ground.*
▶ boggy marshy spongy
←➔ An opposite is **hard**.
5 *There was soft music playing in the background.*
▶ quiet gentle low soothing restful
←➔ An opposite is **loud**.

soil *noun*
You plant seeds in the soil.
▶ earth ground

soldier *noun*
They have sent soldiers to fight the terrorists.
▶ troops *They have sent troops.*
the army *They have sent the army.*

solid *adjective*
1 *The walls are solid.*
▶ dense rigid strong
←➔ An opposite is **hollow**.
2 *Water becomes solid when it freezes.*
▶ hard firm
←➔ An opposite is **soft**.

solve *verb*
Have you solved the puzzle yet?
▶ to work out to figure out to crack to find an answer to
Have you found an answer to the puzzle yet?

song *noun*
1 *As he walked along he sang a little song.*
  ▶ **a tune   a ditty**
2 *What is your country's national song?*
  ▶ **an anthem**
3 *She sang a song to make the baby sleep.*
  ▶ **a lullaby**

sore *adjective*
1 *My throat is sore.*
  ▶ **hurting   painful**
2 *I've got a sore knee.*
  ▶ **painful   aching   throbbing   cut   bruised**
3 *It's sore when I touch it.*
  ▶ **tender**
4 *The cut on his head looked very sore.*
  ▶ **red   raw   painful   nasty**

sorry *adjective*
1 *He was sorry when he saw the damage he had done.*
  ▶ **apologetic   ashamed   upset   remorseful**
  ← → An opposite is **unrepentant**.

> **❝ ❞** ANOTHER WAY OF SAYING *He said sorry.*
>   *He apologized.*

2 *I feel sorry for the little girl.*
  ▶ **sympathetic** *I feel sympathetic towards the little girl.*
  ← → An opposite is **unsympathetic**.

> **❝ ❞** ANOTHER WAY OF SAYING *I feel sorry for her.*
>   *I pity her.*

sort *noun*
1 *What sort of sandwich do you want?*
  ▶ **a type   a kind   a variety**
2 *A terrier is a sort of dog.*
  ▶ **a breed**
3 *A ladybird is a sort of beetle.*
  ▶ **a species**
4 *What sort of trainers do you want to buy?*
  ▶ **a brand   a make**

a
b
c
d
e
f
g
h
i
j
k
l
m
n
o
p
q
r
s
t
u
v
w
x
y
z

a
b
c
d
e
f
g
h
i
j
k
l
m
n
o
p
q
r
s
t
u
v
w
x
y
z

sort *verb*
We sorted the books into three different piles.
▶ to arrange   to group   to organize

sound *noun*
I heard a strange sound coming from the kitchen.
▶ a noise

SOME LOUD SOUNDS

bang	boom	buzz	clang
clank	clatter	crash	pop
rattle	ring	roar	rumble
thud	thump		

SOME GENTLE SOUNDS

bleep	click	drip	fizz
hum	plop	splash	tick
whirr	whistle		

sour *adjective*
Lemon has a sour taste.
▶ bitter   sharp   acid   tart
◀ ▶ An opposite is **sweet**.

space *noun*
1 *Is there enough space for me there?*
▶ room
2 *We squeezed through a space between the two rocks.*
▶ a gap   a hole   an opening

spacecraft *noun*
I would love to go in a spacecraft.
▶ a spaceship   a rocket   a space shuttle

spare *adjective*
Remember to take a spare pair of shoes.
▶ extra   additional

sparkle *verb*
The sea sparkled in the sunlight.
▶ to shine   to glisten   to shimmer   to glint

speak *verb*
Everyone started to speak at once.
▶ **to talk   to say something   to start a conversation**

special *adjective*
1 *Your birthday is a very special day.*
▶ **important   significant**
2 *I've got my own special mug.*
▶ **personal   individual   particular**
←→ An opposite is **ordinary**.

spectacular *adjective*
We watched a spectacular fireworks display.
▶ **exciting   impressive   magnificent   wonderful**

speech *noun*
The winner had to give a speech.
▶ **a talk   a lecture**

speed *noun*
1 *We were walking at a fairly average speed.*
▶ **a pace**
2 *The pilot told us the height and speed of the aeroplane.*
▶ **velocity**
3 *They worked with amazing speed.*
▶ **quickness   swiftness   haste**

speed *verb*
A sports car sped past us.
▶ **to shoot   to zoom   to whizz   to flash**

spell *noun*
She was under a magic spell.
▶ **an enchantment   a charm**

spend *verb*
I've already spent all my pocket money.
▶ **to use**
to pay out *I paid out a lot of money for that jacket.*

spike *noun*
There were spikes along the top of the railings.
▶ **a point**

spill *verb*

1 *Mind you don't spill your drink.*
▶ to drop   to knock over   to upset

2 *She spilt milk all over the kitchen floor.*
▶ to drop   to pour   to tip

3 *Some water had spilt on to the floor.*
▶ to drip   to leak   to splash

4 *Water was spilling over the edge of the bath.*
▶ to pour   to run   to stream   to gush   to splash

spin *verb*

1 *I spun round when I heard his voice.*
▶ to turn   to whirl   to swivel

2 *We watched the dancers spinning across the floor.*
▶ to twirl   to pirouette

3 *The back wheel of my bike was still spinning.*
▶ to turn   to revolve   to rotate   to go round

spirit *noun*

The house is supposed to be haunted by evil spirits.
▶ a ghost   a phantom

spiteful *adjective*

That was a very spiteful thing to do.
▶ nasty   unkind   horrible   mean
← → An opposite is **kind**.

splash *verb*

1 *They splashed us with water.*
▶ to shower   to spray   to squirt   to spatter

2 *They splashed water all over the floor.*
▶ to spill   to slop   to slosh

split *verb*

1 *He split the log with an axe.*
▶ to cut   to chop

2 *The bag split open and all the shopping fell out.*
▶ to break   to tear   to rip

3 *We split the chocolate between us.*
▶ to share   to divide

spoil verb

1 *The water had spoilt some of the books.*
   ▶ to damage   to ruin
2 *The bad weather spoilt our holiday.*
   ▶ to ruin   to mess up

sport noun

Do you enjoy sport?
   ▶ exercise   games

••• SOME TEAM SPORTS

baseball	basketball	cricket
football	hockey	ice hockey
netball	rounders	rugby
volleyball		

SOME INDIVIDUAL SPORTS

athletics	badminton	canoeing
fishing	golf	gymnastics
ice skating	jogging	judo
karate	skiing	snooker
swimming	table tennis	tae kwondo
tennis	trampolining	

---

spot noun

1 *Leopards have dark spots on their bodies.*
   ▶ a mark   a dot   a blotch   a patch
2 *Teenagers often get spots on their faces.*
   ▶ a pimple
   acne (*a lot of spots*)   *Some teenagers get very bad acne.*
3 *When you have chickenpox you get spots all over your body.*
   ▶ a rash
4 *There were a few spots of paint on the floor.*
   ▶ a mark   a dot   a drop   a blob   a smear
   a smudge
5 *We found a lovely spot for a picnic.*
   ▶ a place   a site   a location

spray *verb*
1 *He sprayed some water on to the plants.*
  ▶ to splash   to sprinkle   to squirt
2 *She sprayed us with water.*
  ▶ to splash   to shower   to squirt   to spatter

spread *verb*
1 *The bird spread its wings and flew away.*
  ▶ to open   to stretch out
2 *We spread a cloth on the ground.*
  ▶ to lay out   to unfold   to open out
3 *I spread some jam on to the bread.*
  ▶ to put   to smear

spring *verb*
The cat crouched, ready to spring on the mouse.
  ▶ to jump   to leap   to pounce

squabble *verb*
Those children are always squabbling.
  ▶ to argue   to quarrel   to fight   to fall out   to bicker
    to disagree

squash *verb*
1 *Mind you don't squash those flowers.*
  ▶ to crush   to flatten   to damage   to break
2 *We all squashed into the back of the car.*
  ▶ to squeeze   to crowd
3 *I squashed everything into the suitcase.*
  ▶ to push   to shove   to cram   to squeeze   to jam

squeeze *verb*
1 *We all squeezed into the tiny room.*
  ▶ to squash   to crowd
2 *I squeezed everything into the box.*
  ▶ to push   to shove   to squash   to cram   to jam

squirt *verb*
   1 *Water squirted out of the hole.*
      ▶ to spurt   to gush   to spray
   2 *She squirted water at me.*
      ▶ to spray   to splash

stable *adjective*
   Be careful, the ladder's not very stable.
      ▶ steady   firm   secure

stack *noun*
   I've got a whole stack of books to read.
      ▶ a heap   a pile   a mound

stage *noun*
   We have finished the first stage of our journey.
      ▶ a part   a phase

stain *noun*
   Her shirt was covered in stains.
      ▶ a mark   a spot   a smudge   a smear

stairs *noun*
   She ran down the stairs.
      ▶ steps

stale *adjective*
   All we had to eat was water and stale bread.
      ▶ old   dry   mouldy
   ←→ An opposite is **fresh**.

stand *verb*
   1 *We all stood when the visitors arrived.*
      ▶ to get up
      to get to your feet *We all got to our feet.*
      to rise *We all rose.*
   2 *I can't stand this noise!*
      ▶ to bear   to put up with   to tolerate

standard

standard *noun*

The standard of your work has improved this term.
▶ level   quality

stare *verb*

Why is that boy staring at me?
▶ to look   to gaze   to gape   to glare

start *verb*

1 What time does the film start?
▶ to begin   to commence
2 We're going to start a chess club.
▶ to set up   to create   to establish
3 She started the engine.
▶ to switch on   to turn on
4 We won't start until after lunch.
▶ to set off   to get going   to leave   to set out
←→ An opposite is **finish**.

start *noun*

When is the start of the football season?
▶ the beginning
←→ An opposite is **end**.

statue *noun*

In the main hall is a statue of a woman.
▶ a carving   a sculpture
   a bust (a statue of someone's head and shoulders)

stay *verb*

1 Stay here until I come back.
▶ to remain   to wait
2 Stay on this path until you reach the river.
▶ to continue   to carry on
3 I'm going to stay with my grandma.
▶ to visit
4 I hope it stays dry this afternoon.
▶ to remain

a
b
c
d
e
f
g
h
i
j
k
l
m
n
o
p
q
r
s
t
u
v
w
x
y
z

244

steady *adjective*

1 *Make sure the ladder is steady.*
  ▶ firm stable secure
  ←→ An opposite is **wobbly**.
2 *The music had a steady rhythm.*
  ▶ even regular constant
  ←→ An opposite is **irregular**.

steal *verb*

Someone's stolen my purse.
  ▶ to take to pinch to nick

steep *adjective*

There was a steep drop down to the river.
  ▶ sharp vertical sheer
  ←→ An opposite is **gradual**.

step *noun*

1 *He took a step forwards.*
  ▶ a pace a stride
2 *I climbed up the steps.*
  ▶ stairs

stick *noun*

1 *We collected some sticks to make a fire.*
  ▶ a twig a branch
2 *The tent is held up by sticks.*
  ▶ a pole a rod a cane
3 *Runners in a relay race have to pass a stick to each other.*
  ▶ a baton
4 *Police officers carry special sticks.*
  ▶ a truncheon
5 *The giant carried a large stick.*
  ▶ a club
6 *He uses a stick to help him walk.*
  ▶ a walking stick a crutch

a
b
c
d
e
f
g
h
i
j
k
l
m
n
o
p
q
r
s
t
u
v
w
x
y
z

245

stick

stick *verb*

1 *I stuck the pictures in my book.*
► to glue   to fix

2 *Sometimes the door sticks a bit.*
► to jam   to get stuck

3 *She stuck a pin into my arm.*
► to jab   to stab

sticky *adjective*
She picked up some of the sticky mixture.
► gooey   tacky   gluey

stiff *adjective*

1 *Use a piece of stiff cardboard for the base of the model.*
► hard   rigid
←→ An opposite is **soft**.

2 *Mix the ingredients together to make a stiff paste.*
► thick   firm
←→ An opposite is **soft**.

3 *The door handle was a bit stiff.*
► stuck   jammed   difficult to move

4 *I woke up with a stiff neck.*
► sore   painful

still *adjective*

1 *It was a very still evening.*
► quiet   calm   peaceful

2 *We all stood perfectly still.*
► motionless

stir *verb*
She stirred the mixture with a spoon.
► to mix   to beat   to whisk

stomach *noun*
I've got a pain in my stomach.
► tummy   belly

stone *noun*
He threw a stone into the water.
► a pebble   a rock   a boulder (*a very big stone*)

stop *verb*

1 *The policeman stopped the traffic.*
▸ **to halt   to hold up**

2 *The bus stopped outside the school.*
▸ **to pull up   to draw up   to park   to come to a halt**
   to grind to a halt   to come to a standstill

3 *He stopped for a moment.*
▸ **to hesitate   to pause   to wait**

4 *Shall we stop for lunch?*
▸ **to break off   to knock off**

5 *The baby finally stopped crying.*
▸ **to finish   to quit**

6 *Most children eventually stop sucking their thumb.*
▸ **to give up   to grow out of**

7 *This silly behaviour has got to stop.*
▸ **to end   to finish   to come to an end   to cease**

8 *It is time to stop this nonsense.*
▸ **to put an end to   to put a stop to**

9 *We must stop him from getting away.*
▸ **to prevent**

store *verb*

We can store all these boxes in the garage.
▸ **to keep   to put away**

storm *noun*

That night there was a terrible storm.
▸ **a thunderstorm   a rain storm   a gale   a hurricane**
   a tornado
   a blizzard (*a storm with snow*)

story *noun*

He told us a story about a fox.
▸ **a tale   a yarn**

●●● SOME TYPES OF STORY

an adventure story	**a fairy tale**	**a folk tale**
a legend	**a myth**	**a parable**
a traditional tale		

---

a
b
c
d
e
f
g
h
i
j
k
l
m
n
o
p
q
r
s
t
u
v
w
x
y
z

straight *adjective*
That picture isn't straight.
▸ level   upright
←→ An opposite is **crooked**.

strain *verb*
1 *I had to strain to reach the handle.*
▸ to struggle   to try hard   to make an effort
2 *I strained a muscle when I was running.*
▸ to hurt   to injure   to damage

strange *adjective*
1 *What a strange animal!*
▸ funny   peculiar   odd   curious
←→ An opposite is **normal**.
2 *When I woke up I was in a strange place.*
▸ different   new   unfamiliar   unknown
←→ An opposite is **familiar**.

stream *noun*
We paddled across the stream.
▸ a brook   a river

street *noun*
That boy lives in the same street as me.
▸ a road   an avenue

strength *noun*
I had to use all my strength to open the door.
▸ force   might   power

stretch *verb*
You can stretch elastic.
▸ to pull out   to lengthen   to extend

strict *adjective*
Our teacher is quite strict.
▸ harsh   severe   stern   firm

string *noun*
> We tied the parcel up with string.
> ▶ cord   rope   twine   ribbon

strip *verb*
> He stripped and got into the bath.
> ▶ to undress   to take your clothes off

stripe *noun*
> She was wearing a blue dress with white stripes.
> ▶ a line   a band

strong *adjective*
> **1** You have to be very strong to be a firefighter.
> ▶ tough   muscular   brawny   strapping
> **2** I wish I had strong arms.
> ▶ powerful   muscular
> **3** She's been very ill, and she's not strong enough to go outside yet.
> ▶ well   fit   healthy
> **4** The rope wasn't strong enough to hold my weight.
> ▶ tough   thick
> **5** The roof must be made of a strong material.
> ▶ tough   solid   hard-wearing   durable   unbreakable   indestructible
> **6** The shelter they had built was quite strong.
> ▶ well-made   well-built
> **7** This orange squash is too strong.
> ▶ concentrated
> ◀ ➔ An opposite is **weak**.

struggle *verb*
> **1** The thief struggled to get away.
> ▶ to fight   to wrestle
> **2** We were struggling to carry all the boxes.
> ▶ to try hard   to work hard

a
b
c
d
e
f
g
h
i
j
k
l
m
n
o
p
q
r
s
t
u
v
w
x
y
z

stubborn adjective

He was stubborn and refused to come with us.
▶ **obstinate defiant wilful disobedient**

study verb

1 *We're studying the Romans at school.*
▶ **to learn about to read about**
2 *He studied the map carefully.*
▶ **to look at to examine**

stuff noun

1 *There was some sticky stuff on the floor.*
▶ **a substance** *There was a sticky substance on the floor.*
2 *We cleared all the old stuff out of the cupboards.*
▶ **things odds and ends bits and pieces**
3 *Don't forget to take all your stuff with you.*
▶ **things belongings possessions kit**

stuffy adjective

The room was stuffy.
▶ **warm airless**
◀▶ An opposite is **airy**.

stumble verb

I stumbled over a big stone.
▶ **to trip to slip to lose your balance**

stupid adjective

1 *That was a stupid thing to do!*
▶ **silly daft foolish unwise**
2 *You must be stupid if you believe that!*
▶ **daft dim dense brainless thick**
◀▶ An opposite is **intelligent**.

style noun

1 *I like the colour of those trousers, but I don't like the style.*
▶ **a design**
2 *She likes wearing the latest styles.*
▶ **a fashion**

subject *noun*

I want to choose an interesting subject for my project.
▶ **a topic   a theme**

subtract *verb*

Can you subtract 6 from 9?
▶ **to take away   to deduct**
   to find the difference between *Can you find the difference between 6 and 9?*

succeed *verb*

1 *I finally succeeded in getting the door open.*
▶ **to manage** *I managed to get the door open.*
   to be able to *I was able to get the door open.*
2 *She wants to become a pilot, but I don't know if she'll succeed.*
▶ **to be successful**
3 *All children should try to succeed at school.*
▶ **to do well**
4 *Did your plan succeed?*
▶ **to work   to be successful** *Was your plan successful?*
←→ An opposite is **fail**.

success *noun*

The concert was a great success.
▶ **a triumph   a hit**
←→ An opposite is **failure**.

sudden *adjective*

1 *There was a sudden change in the weather.*
▶ **unexpected   abrupt**
2 *He made a sudden dash for the door.*
▶ **quick   swift**

suddenly

1 *I realized suddenly that I was lost.*
▶ **all of a sudden**
2 *A man appeared suddenly from behind the door.*
▶ **unexpectedly   without warning**

suffer *verb*

I hate to see animals suffering.
▶ **to be in pain** *I hate to see animals in pain.*

a
b
c
d
e
f
g
h
i
j
k
l
m
n
o
p
q
r
s
t
u
v
w
x
y
z

suggest *verb*
I suggested that we should go back home.
▶ to propose   to advise   to recommend

suggestion *noun*
What do you think we should do? What's your suggestion?
▶ an idea   a proposal   a plan

suit *verb*
That dress really suits you.
▶ to look nice on *That dress looks nice on you.*
to look right on *That dress looks right on you.*

suitable *adjective*
Is this dress suitable for a wedding?
▶ appropriate   right
← → An opposite is **unsuitable**.

sulk *verb*
Is Tom still sulking?
▶ to be in a mood *Is Tom still in a mood?*

sulky *adjective*
He's been sulky all afternoon.
▶ moody   sullen   bad-tempered   grumpy

sunny *adjective*
It was a lovely sunny day.
▶ bright   fine   clear   cloudless
← → An opposite is **cloudy**.

super *adjective*
That's a super painting!
▶ wonderful   marvellous   brilliant   fabulous   fantastic
superb

supply *noun*
There's a supply of paper in the cupboard.
▶ a store   a stock   a reserve

support *verb*
1 *Those pillars support the roof.*
▶ to hold up   to prop up
2 *You should support your friends when they are in trouble.*
▶ to help   to stand up for   to stick up for
3 *We went to support our team.*
▶ to encourage   to cheer on

suppose *verb*
1 *I suppose we ought to go home now.*
▶ to think   to guess   to reckon
2 *I suppose she must be the new teacher.*
▶ to assume   to presume

sure *adjective*
1 *I'm sure she lives somewhere round here.*
▶ certain   positive   convinced   confident
2 *He's sure to remember.*
▶ bound
←→ An opposite is **unsure**.

surprise *noun*
1 *Winning the competition was a complete surprise.*
▶ a shock   a bolt from the blue
2 *He looked at me in surprise.*
▶ amazement   astonishment

surprise *verb*
It surprised everyone when our team won the game.
▶ to amaze   to astonish   to astound   to shock

surprised *adjective*
I was really surprised when I saw all the presents.
▶ amazed   astonished   astounded   staggered   flabbergasted   shocked

surrender *verb*
After a long fight, the army surrendered.
▶ to give in   to capitulate   to yield

a b c d e f g h i j k l m n o p q r **s** t u v w x y z

a
b
c
d
e
f
g
h
i
j
k
l
m
n
o
p
q
r
s
t
u
v
w
x
y
z

survive *verb*
A lot of people were killed in the explosion, and only a few survived.
▶ **to live   to stay alive**

suspect *verb*
I suspect that he is not telling the truth.
▶ **to think   to believe   to guess**
to have a feeling *I have a feeling that he is not telling the truth.*
to have a hunch *I have a hunch that he is not telling the truth.*

swamp *noun*
We didn't want to get lost in the swamp.
▶ **a bog   a marsh**

swear *verb*
1 *I swear I didn't touch your pen!*
▶ **to promise**
to give your word *I give you my word that I didn't touch your pen.*
2 *He swore he would never do it again.*
▶ **to promise   to vow**
3 *The teacher told him off because he swore.*
▶ **to use bad language   to curse**

sweep *verb*
I swept the floor.
▶ **to brush**

sweet *adjective*
1 *This orange juice is too sweet.*
▶ **sugary**
←→ An opposite is **bitter**.
2 *That little dog is really sweet!*
▶ **lovely   lovable   cute   adorable**
←→ An opposite is **ugly**.

swim *verb*
We swam in the river.
▶ **to bathe   to go swimming**

swing *verb*

   1 *The loose rope was swinging backwards and forwards.*
     ▶ **to sway   to wave**

   2 *The monkey was swinging from a branch.*
     ▶ **to hang   to dangle**

switch *noun*

   Don't touch any of those switches.
     ▶ **a button   a knob   a control**

switch *verb*

   I switched the light on.
     ▶ **to turn**

swoop *verb*

   The owl swooped down on its prey.
     ▶ **to dive   to drop**
     to descend *The owl descended on its prey.*

sympathy *noun*

   Everyone gave me a lot of sympathy when I was ill.
     ▶ **compassion   understanding   pity**

a
b
c
d
e
f
g
h
i
j
k
l
m
n
o
p
q
r
s
t
u
v
w
x
y
z

a
b
c
d
e
f
g
h
i
j
k
l
m
n
o
p
q
r
s
t
u
v
w
x
y
z

Tt

take *verb*
1 *I offered him a sweet and he took one.*
▶ to pick up   to grab   to snatch
2 *She took my hand and led me away.*
▶ to hold   to take hold of   to grasp
3 *Don't forget to take your lunch.*
▶ to carry   to bring
4 *The nurse took us to the ward.*
▶ to lead   to accompany   to guide
5 *Dad took us to the station in his car.*
▶ to transport
to give someone a lift. *Dad gave us a lift in his car.*
6 *The burglar took the jewels.*
▶ to steal   to pinch   to seize   to run off with
7 *Can you take 5 from 16?*
▶ to subtract   to deduct

take off *verb*
I took off my coat.
▶ to remove   to slip off

take out *verb*
The dentist took out one of my teeth.
▶ to remove   to pull out   to extract

talent *noun*
He's a young tennis player with a lot of talent.
▶ ability   skill   flair

talented *adjective*
He is a very talented musician.
▶ clever   gifted   skilful   able

talk *noun*
I had a talk with my teacher.
▶ a chat   a conversation   a discussion

talk *verb*
1 We talked about our hobbies.
▶ to chat   to have a conversation   to have a discussion
2 The teacher told us to stop talking.
▶ to chat   to chatter   to natter   to gossip
3 Animals can talk to each other in different ways.
▶ to speak   to communicate

tall *adjective*
1 She is quite tall for her age.
▶ big
← → An opposite is **short**.
2 There are some very tall buildings in the city centre.
▶ big   high   lofty
← → An opposite is **low**.

tame *adjective*
The animals in the zoo are all very tame.
▶ gentle   docile   safe
← → An opposite is **wild**.

tangled *adjective*
The string was all tangled.
▶ knotted   twisted

tap *verb*
She tapped on the door.
▶ to knock   to rap

taste *noun*
1 The ice cream had a lovely creamy taste.
▶ a flavour
2 Can I have a taste of your chocolate?
▶ a bit   a piece   a mouthful   a nibble
3 He let me have a taste of his orange juice.
▶ a sip   a mouthful

a
b
c
d
e
f
g
h
i
j
k
l
m
n
o
p
q
r
s

t

u
v
w
x
y
z

taste *verb*
Would you like to taste my drink?
▶ **to try   to sample**

teach *verb*
1 *A teacher's job is to teach children.*
▶ **to educate**
2 *My brother taught me how to use the computer.*
▶ **to show   to tell**
to train *He trained us to use the computer.*
3 *Our football coach teaches us how to play football.*
▶ **to coach   to train**

tear *verb*
Be careful you don't tear your dress.
▶ **to rip   to split**

tease *verb*
Sometimes my friends tease me.
▶ **to make fun of   to laugh at   to torment   to taunt**

telephone *verb*
I'll telephone you later.
▶ **to phone   to call   to ring**
to give someone a ring *I'll give you a ring later.*

tell *verb*
1 *He told me he'd be home for tea.*
▶ **to say** *He said he'd be home for tea.*
to promise *He promised he'd be home for tea.*
2 *Please tell me if you are going to be late.*
▶ **to let someone know** *Please let me know if you are going to be late.*
3 *My dad told me how to use a calculator.*
▶ **to show   to teach**
to explain *He explained to me how to use a calculator.*
4 *You should tell the police if you see anything unusual.*
▶ **to inform   to notify**

▶▶

5 *She finally told me the secret.*
> ▶ **to reveal** *She revealed the secret to me.*

6 *My dad told us a story.*
> ▶ **to relate** *He related a story.*
> **to narrate** *He narrated a story to us.*

7 *Can you tell us what happened?*
> ▶ **to describe** *Can you describe what happened?*
> **to recount** *Can you recount what happened?*

8 *Mum told us to stop shouting.*
> ▶ **to order to instruct to command**

tell off *verb*
The teacher told us off.
> ▶ **to scold to reprimand to rebuke**

temper *noun*
1 *You seem to be in a very good temper today.*
> ▶ **mood humour**

2 *The man was in a terrible temper!*
> ▶ **a rage a fury**

> **" "** OTHER WAYS OF SAYING *He was in a bad temper.*
> *He was angry.*
> *He was bad-tempered.*
> *He was grumpy.*

terrible *adjective*
1 *The weather was terrible!*
> ▶ **awful dreadful horrible ghastly**

2 *This is terrible news!*
> ▶ **bad sad awful shocking upsetting**

3 *I'm a terrible tennis player.*
> ▶ **hopeless useless**

terrific *adjective*
I think that's a terrific idea!
> ▶ **wonderful brilliant excellent fantastic**

terrified *adjective*
I was absolutely terrified!
▶ petrified

terrify *verb*
The thought of singing in front of all those people would terrify me.
▶ to frighten   to scare   to petrify

terror *noun*
People ran away from the fire in terror.
▶ fear   fright   panic

test *noun*
We've got a spelling test tomorrow.
▶ an exam   an examination

test *verb*
Now we must test the machine to see if it works.
▶ to try   to try out   to use

thank *verb*
I thanked them for their present.
▶ to say thank you
to express your gratitude *I expressed my gratitude.*
to show your appreciation *I showed my appreciation.*

thaw *verb*
1 *The snow has started to thaw.*
▶ to melt
2 *I took the meat out of the freezer so that it would thaw.*
▶ to defrost   to warm up

thick *adjective*
1 *He drew a thick line.*
▶ wide   broad
2 *The castle had thick stone walls.*
▶ solid   strong
3 *She cut herself a thick slice of cake.*
▶ big   large   fat

▶▶

4 We had to walk through thick mud.
▶ **deep**
5 He was wearing a thick coat.
▶ **heavy   warm**
←→ An opposite is **thin**.

thief *noun*
The police have caught the thieves.
▶ **a robber   a burglar**
a pickpocket (*someone who steals things from people's pockets*)
a mugger (*someone who robs people in the street*)
a shoplifter (*someone who steals things from shops*)

thin *adjective*
1 She drew a thin line.
▶ **fine   narrow**
←→ An opposite is **thick**.
2 My sister is very thin.
▶ **slim   slender   skinny**
←→ An opposite is **fat**.
3 This paint is too thin.
▶ **watery   runny   diluted**
←→ An opposite is **thick**.
4 She was only wearing a thin cotton dress.
▶ **light   flimsy**
←→ An opposite is **thick**.

thing *noun*
1 We found some very interesting things in the attic.
▶ **an object   an article   an item**
2 A corkscrew is a thing for opening bottles.
▶ **a tool   a device   a gadget   a machine**
3 A very strange thing happened to me today.
▶ **an event   an incident**
4 We had to do some very difficult things.
▶ **an action   an act   a job   a task**
5 He's only got one thing on his mind.
▶ **an idea   a thought**

a b c d e f g h i j k l m n o p q r s t u v w x y z

think

think *verb*

1 *Think before you act.*
   ▶ **to concentrate** **to use your mind**
2 *He was sitting in a chair just thinking.*
   ▶ **to meditate** **to muse** **to daydream**
3 *I was thinking about all the things that had happened the day before.*
   ▶ **to reflect on** *I reflected on what had happened.*
   to mull over *I mulled over what had happened.*
   to ponder *I pondered over what had happened.*
4 *He was still thinking about what to do next.*
   ▶ **to consider** *He was considering what to do next.*
   to plan *He was planning what he would do next.*
5 *Think how you would have felt.*
   ▶ **to picture** **to imagine** **to visualize**
6 *Try not to think about the dangers.*
   ▶ **to worry**
7 *I think that you are right.*
   ▶ **to believe** **to reckon**

thoroughly *adverb*

1 *Make sure you clean everything thoroughly.*
   ▶ **carefully** **properly**
2 *I was thoroughly exhausted.*
   ▶ **completely** **totally** **utterly** **absolutely**

thought *noun*

I've just had an interesting thought.
   ▶ **an idea** **a brainwave**

thoughtful *adjective*

1 *He was sitting on his own, looking thoughtful.*
   ▶ **serious** **pensive** **reflective**
2 *You should try to be more thoughtful.*
   ▶ **considerate** **kind** **helpful** **unselfish**
   ← → An opposite is **thoughtless**.

thrilling *adjective*

Going on the big rides was a thrilling experience.
   ▶ **exciting** **electrifying**

throw *verb*
1 *She threw a stone and broke the glass.*
▸ to fling to hurl to sling to toss to lob to chuck
2 *He threw the ball towards the batsman.*
▸ to bowl

throw away *verb*
My old shoes didn't fit me any more so I threw them away.
▸ to throw out to get rid of to dispose of to discard to dump

tidy *adjective*
1 *Make sure your bedroom is tidy.*
▸ neat shipshape spick and span
2 *The children all looked tidy.*
▸ neat smart well-groomed
3 *I'm not a tidy person.*
▸ neat organized house-proud
←→ An opposite is **untidy**.

tie *verb*
1 *I can't tie my shoelaces.*
▸ to do up to fasten
2 *She wound some string round the parcel and tied it tightly.*
▸ to knot
3 *Why don't you tie the two bits together?*
▸ to fasten to join to fix
4 *They tied the boat to a post.*
▸ to fasten to secure to moor
5 *He tied the animal to the fence.*
▸ to tether

tight *adjective*
1 *My trousers are a bit tight.*
▸ small tight-fitting close-fitting
2 *Make sure the jar has a tight lid.*
▸ firm secure
3 *Pull the rope until it is tight.*
▸ stretched taut
←→ An opposite is **loose**.

a
b
c
d
e
f
g
h
i
j
k
l
m
n
o
p
q
r
s
t
u
v
w
x
y
z

time *noun*

1 *He sat in silence for a long time.*
▶ **a while   a period**

> 66 99 **OTHER WAYS OF SAYING** *We had to wait for a long time.*
> *We had to wait for ages.*
> *We had to wait for hours.*
>
> **OTHER WAYS OF SAYING** *It will only take a short time.*
> *It will only take a minute.*
> *It will only take a moment.*

2 *The 1950s was a very interesting time.*
▶ **a period   an era   an age**
3 *I waited for a good time to ask for more pocket money.*
▶ **a moment   an opportunity**

tiny *adjective*
Some insects are tiny.
▶ **minute   minuscule   microscopic**
←→ An opposite is **big**.

tip *noun*
1 *She stood up on the tips of her toes.*
▶ **the end   the point**
2 *We could only see the tip of the iceberg.*
▶ **the top**

tip *verb*
1 *I could feel the bench beginning to tip back.*
▶ **to lean   to tilt**
2 *She tipped water all over the floor.*
▶ **to pour   to spill   to slop**

tip over *verb*
The boat tipped over in the rough sea.
▶ **to capsize   to overturn**

tired *adjective*

1 *We were tired after our walk.*
   ► **exhausted   weary   worn out   sleepy**
2 *I'm tired of this game.*
   ► **fed up** *I'm fed up with this game.*
   bored *I'm bored with this game.*

toilet *noun*

Can I use your toilet, please?
   ► **a lavatory   a WC   a loo**

tool *noun*

You can use a special tool to get the lid off.
   ► **a device   a gadget   an implement**

••• SOME TOOLS FOR WOODWORK

| a drill | a hammer | a plane |
| pliers | a screwdriver | a spanner |

SOME TOOLS YOU USE IN THE GARDEN

a fork	a hoe	a rake
shears	a spade	a trowel
a watering can		

---

top *noun*

1 *We climbed to the top of the mountain.*
   ► **the summit**
2 *We could see the tops of the mountains in the distance.*
   ► **a peak   a tip**
3 *We drove over the top of the hill.*
   ► **the crest**
4 *Put the top back on the jar.*
   ► **a lid   a cover   a cap**
   ← → An opposite is **bottom**.

topic *noun*

The topic we are studying this term is food.
   ► **a subject   a theme**

a
b
c
d
e
f
g
h
i
j
k
l
m
n
o
p
q
r
s
t
u
v
w
x
y
z

torment *verb*
Stop tormenting your brother!
▶ to tease   to bully   to annoy

total *adjective*
1 *What will the total cost be?*
▶ full   whole
2 *Because it rained, the picnic was a total disaster.*
▶ complete   absolute

total *noun*
Count the money and tell me the total.
▶ the answer

totally *adverb*
My new bike was totally ruined!
▶ completely   absolutely   utterly

touch *verb*
1 *He touched my arm.*
▶ to pat   to tap   to stroke   to brush
2 *You mustn't touch the things on display in the museum.*
▶ to handle   to hold   to feel
3 *Please don't touch the controls.*
▶ to fiddle with   to mess about with   to play with

tough *adjective*
1 *The rope is made of very tough nylon.*
▶ strong   hard-wearing   unbreakable
2 *He thinks he's a really tough guy.*
▶ strong   hard   rough   violent
←→ An opposite is **weak**.

tradition *noun*
Having a cake on your birthday is a tradition.
▶ a custom

traffic *noun*
There was a lot of traffic on the road.
▶ cars lorries buses coaches vans vehicles

tragedy *noun*
The plane crash was a terrible tragedy.
▶ a disaster a catastrophe a calamity

train *verb*
1 *Mr Grout trains our football team.*
▶ to coach to instruct
2 *He trained his dog to beg for sweets.*
▶ to teach
3 *Our team trains every Thursday.*
▶ to practise

trap *noun*
The poor rabbit got caught in a trap.
▶ a snare

trap *verb*
We trapped the smugglers in the cave.
▶ stuck caught cornered

travel *verb*
We travelled all around the world.
▶ to go to journey to tour to drive to sail to fly to walk
  to ride to cycle to hitch-hike

tread *verb*
Mind you don't tread on the flowers.
▶ to step to walk to stand to trample to stamp

treasure *noun*
We found a box of buried treasure.
▶ gold silver jewels riches

a
b
c
d
e
f
g
h
i
j
k
l
m
n
o
p
q
r
s
t
u
v
w
x
y
z

tree *noun*

• • • SOME TYPES OF DECIDUOUS TREE

ash	beech	birch
elm	hawthorn	hazel
horse chestnut	larch	maple
oak	poplar	sycamore
willow		

SOME TYPES OF EVERGREEN TREE

fir	holly	palm
pine	yew	

---

tremble *verb*
I was trembling with fear.
▶ to shake   to quake   to quiver   to shiver   to shudder

tremendous *adjective*
1 *The machines make a tremendous noise.*
   ▶ great   huge   terrific
2 *We had a tremendous time.*
   ▶ great   wonderful   fantastic   excellent

trick *noun*
1 *We played a trick on our friends.*
   ▶ a joke   a prank   a hoax
2 *The dolphins did some amazing tricks.*
   ▶ a stunt

trick *verb*
He tricked us into giving him our money.
   ▶ to cheat   to fool   to swindle   to con

trickle *verb*
Water trickled out of the tap.
   ▶ to drip   to dribble   to leak   to seep

trip *noun*
We went on a trip to the seaside.
   ▶ an outing   an excursion   a journey   a visit   an expedition

trip *verb*
I tripped and fell.
> ▶ **to stumble   to slip**
> **to lose your balance** *I lost my balance.*

trouble *noun*
1 *We've had a lot of trouble with our new computer.*
> ▶ **difficulties   problems**
2 *She's had a lot of troubles recently.*
> ▶ **cares   distress   worry   suffering**
3 *There was some trouble in the playground at lunchtime.*
> ▶ **bother   fighting**
4 *Now go off and play and don't get into trouble.*
> ▶ **mischief**

true *adjective*
1 *The film is based on a true story.*
> ▶ **real   genuine   actual**
2 *What he said isn't true.*
> ▶ **correct   accurate   right**
← → An opposite is **made-up**.

trust *verb*
1 *I don't trust that man.*
> ▶ **to have confidence in**
2 *Can I trust to you get on with your work while I am away?*
> ▶ **to rely on   to depend on   to count on**

try *verb*
1 *I tried to climb over the wall.*
> ▶ **to attempt   to make an effort   to strive**
2 *Can I try the cake?*
> ▶ **to taste   to sample**
3 *Would you like to try my new bike?*
> ▶ **to try out   to test**
> **to have a go** *Would you like to have a go on my new bike?*

tune

tune *noun*
Do you know the words to this tune?
▶ a melody

tunnel *noun*
There is a secret tunnel leading to the castle.
▶ a passage
an underpass (*a tunnel under a road*)

turn *verb*
1 *I turned round to see who was behind me.*
▶ to spin   to whirl   to swivel
2 *I turned the key in the lock.*
▶ to rotate
3 *The wheel began to turn.*
▶ to revolve   to rotate   to spin
4 *In the autumn some leaves turn red.*
▶ to become   to go
5 *Tadpoles turn into frogs.*
▶ to become   to change into
6 *I turned the light on.*
▶ to switch
7 *We turned the attic into a playroom.*
▶ to change   to convert   to transform

turn *noun*
Be patient—it will be your turn in a minute.
▶ a go   a chance   an opportunity

twinkle *verb*
The lights twinkled in the distance.
▶ to shine   to sparkle

twist *verb*
1 *I twisted the wire round the pole.*
▶ to wind   to loop   to coil
2 *She twisted the ribbons together.*
▶ to plait   to wind

type *noun*
1 *What type of music do you like?*
▶ **a kind   a sort**
2 *A collie is a type of dog.*
▶ **a breed**
3 *A ladybird is a type of beetle.*
▶ **a species**
4 *I don't like that type of trainers.*
▶ **a brand   a make**

typical *adjective*
It was a typical winter's day.
▶ **normal   ordinary   average**
←→ An opposite is **unusual**.

Uu

ugly adjective
1 *We screamed when we saw the ugly monster.*
  ▶ **horrible hideous frightful repulsive grotesque**
2 *Two of the sisters were beautiful, but the third was ugly.*
  ▶ **plain unattractive**
←→ An opposite is **beautiful**.

uncomfortable adjective
The bed was very uncomfortable.
  ▶ **hard lumpy**
←→ An opposite is **comfortable**.

unconscious adjective
1 *I was unconscious for a few minutes after the fall.*
  ▶ **knocked out out cold**
2 *The blow knocked him unconscious.*
  ▶ **senseless**
←→ An opposite is **conscious**.

understand verb
Do you understand what I'm saying?
  ▶ **to follow to grasp to see**

undo verb
She undid her shoelaces.
  ▶ **to untie to unfasten**

unemployed adjective
My uncle is unemployed.
  ▶ **out of work on the dole jobless**
←→ An opposite is **employed**.

uneven *adjective*
The road was very uneven.
  ▶ bumpy rough
◄ ➔ An opposite is **smooth**.

unfair *adjective*
1 It's unfair if she gets more than me.
  ▶ wrong unjust unreasonable
2 We complained that the referee was unfair.
  ▶ biased
◄ ➔ An opposite is **fair**.

unfriendly *adjective*
The other children were very unfriendly.
  ▶ unkind nasty hostile rude mean unwelcoming
◄ ➔ An opposite is **friendly**.

unhappy *adjective*
I was unhappy when I didn't get the part in the play.
  ▶ sad upset miserable fed up dejected despondent
  depressed disappointed gloomy glum
  down in the dumps heartbroken
◄ ➔ An opposite is **happy**.

unkind *adjective*
Jo hates to see people being unkind to animals.
  ▶ horrible nasty mean cruel spiteful
◄ ➔ An opposite is **kind**.

unlucky *adjective*
We were unlucky to miss the bus.
  ▶ unfortunate
◄ ➔ An opposite is **lucky**.

unpleasant *adjective*
1 He said some unpleasant things to me.
  ▶ horrible nasty mean unkind rude unfriendly
  upsetting
2 The meat had an unpleasant taste.
  ▶ horrible nasty disgusting revolting terrible
◄ ➔ An opposite is **pleasant**.

a
b
c
d
e
f
g
h
i
j
k
l
m
n
o
p
q
r
s
t
u
v
w
x
y
z

untidy *adjective*
1 *The bedroom is always untidy.*
  ▶ messy chaotic
2 *He always looks untidy.*
  ▶ messy scruffy unkempt
3 *All the clothes were in an untidy pile on the floor.*
  ▶ jumbled muddled
4 *This work is very untidy!*
  ▶ messy careless sloppy
  ← → An opposite is **tidy**.

unusual *adjective*
It's unusual to have snow in May.
  ▶ extraordinary odd peculiar strange surprising
    uncommon
  ← → An opposite is **ordinary**.

upset *adjective*
1 *I was very upset when my cat died.*
  ▶ sad distressed
2 *I felt upset when the other children teased me.*
  ▶ hurt aggrieved

upset *verb*
1 *Seeing the pictures of the war on TV upset me.*
  ▶ to distress to sadden to frighten to scare
    to worry
2 *Some of the things he said really upset me.*
  ▶ to hurt
    to hurt someone's feelings *Some of the things he said hurt my feelings.*

urge *noun*
I had a sudden urge to giggle.
  ▶ a desire a wish a need

use *verb*
1 *They used machines to dig the tunnel.*
  ▶ to employ to make use of
2 *Do you know how to use a pair of scissors?*
  ▶ to handle to manipulate

▶▶

3 *Everyone should learn how to use a computer.*
   ▶ to work   to operate
4 *Have we used all the paint?*
   ▶ to finish

useful *adjective*
1 *Mobile phones are very useful.*
   ▶ handy   practical   convenient
2 *She gave us some very useful advice.*
   ▶ helpful   valuable
← → An opposite is **useless**.

useless *adjective*
1 *This old bicycle is useless!*
   ▶ unusable   worthless
   ← → An opposite is **useful**.
2 *I was a useless goalkeeper.*
   ▶ hopeless   terrible   incompetent
   ← → An opposite is **good**.

usual *adjective*
1 *I went to bed at my usual time of eight o'clock.*
   ▶ normal   ordinary
2 *The usual answer is no.*
   ▶ normal   typical

usually *adverb*
I usually get up at seven o'clock.
   ▶ normally   generally

vague *adjective*
He only gave a vague description of the thief.
▶ **general   unclear   confused   not very detailed**
←→ An opposite is **exact**.

vain *adjective*
He's so vain that he's always looking in the mirror.
▶ **conceited   arrogant   big-headed**
←→ An opposite is **modest**.

valuable *adjective*
Some of these paintings are very valuable.
▶ **expensive   precious**
priceless *Some of these paintings are priceless.*
←→ An opposite is **worthless**.

> **6 9** ANOTHER WAY OF SAYING *Some of these paintings are very valuable.*
> *Some of these paintings are worth a lot of money.*

value *noun*
No one knows the exact value of these jewels.
▶ **the worth   the price**

vanish *verb*
The wizard lifted up his wand and then vanished.
▶ **to disappear**

variety *noun*
1 There is a variety of colours to choose from.
▶ **an assortment   a choice**
2 They sell ten different varieties of ice cream.
▶ **a type   a sort   a kind**

a
b
c
d
e
f
g
h
i
j
k
l
m
n
o
p
q
r
s
t
u
v
w
x
y
z

various *adjective*
There were various things to eat.
▶ different   assorted

vary *verb*
The date of Easter varies each year.
▶ to change
to be different *The date is different each year.*

vegetable *noun*

••• SOME TYPES OF VEGETABLE		
asparagus	aubergines	beans
beetroot	broccoli	cabbage
carrots	cauliflower	celery
courgettes	leeks	mangetout
marrows	okra	onions
parsnips	peas	plantain
potatoes	pumpkins	spinach
sprouts	sweetcorn	tomatoes
turnips	yams	

vibrate *verb*
The whole house vibrates when a lorry goes past.
▶ to shake   to wobble   to rattle   to shudder

victory *noun*
We celebrated our team's victory.
▶ a win   a success   a triumph
←→ An opposite is **defeat**.

villain *noun*
The police caught the villain in the end.
▶ a criminal   a crook   a baddy

violent *adjective*
1 *Sometimes he is quite violent towards other children.*
▶ aggressive   rough
2 *They were the victims of a violent attack.*
▶ ferocious   savage
3 *That night there was a violent storm.*
▶ severe   fierce   raging

visible

visible *adjective*
 Stars are only visible at night.
  ▶ **noticeable   obvious**
 ←→ An opposite is **invisible**.

visit *verb*
 I'm going to visit my grandma next week.
  ▶ **to see   to call on   to stay with**

visitor *noun*
 Are you expecting a visitor?
  ▶ **a guest   a caller**
   company *Are you expecting company?*

volume *noun*
 Please could you turn down the volume on the TV?
  ▶ **the sound   the loudness**

vote for *verb*
 Who did you vote for?
  ▶ **to choose   to pick   to select**

wait verb

1 *Wait here until I get back.*
  ▶ **to stay   to remain   to stop**
2 *Wait a minute, I won't be long.*
  ▶ **to hang on   to hold on**
3 *She waited for a while before she opened the door.*
  ▶ **to pause   to hesitate**

wake up verb

I wake up at seven o'clock.
  ▶ **to awaken   to get up   to rise**

walk verb

> **!!!** **walk** is a word that is often overused.
>
> 1 *I walk to school every morning.*
>   ▶ **to go on foot   to travel on foot**
> 2 *She walked quickly down the street.*
>   ▶ **to stride   to march   to hurry   to rush**
> 3 *We walked slowly along the beach.*
>   ▶ **to wander   to stroll   to amble   to saunter**
> 4 *He was walking around noisily in his heavy boots.*
>   ▶ **to stomp   to clump**
> 5 *She walked very quietly to the door.*
>   ▶ **to creep   to sneak   to tiptoe**
> 6 *He walked unsteadily back to his bed.*
>   ▶ **to limp   to hobble   to shuffle   to stagger   to stumble**
> 7 *The children walked wearily home.*
>   ▶ **to trudge   to plod**
> 8 *He walked proudly around the stage.*
>   ▶ **to strut   to swagger**
> 9 *They walked for three days and nights over the mountains.*
>   ▶ **to hike   to trek**

a b c d e f g h i j k l m n o p q r s t u v **w** x y z

wander *verb*

The sheep wander about the hills.
> ▶ **to roam   to rove**

want *verb*

1 *Do you want an ice cream?*
> ▶ **to fancy   to feel like**

> **6 9** ANOTHER WAY OF SAYING *Do you want an ice cream?*
> *Would you like an ice cream?*

2 *I really want a drink!*
> ▶ **to need   to be dying for   to be desperate for**

3 *She had always wanted a pony of her own.*
> ▶ **to wish for   to long for   to yearn for**

4 *The magic lamp can bring you anything that you want.*
> ▶ **to desire   to wish for**

5 *I want to be a professional footballer.*
> ▶ **to dream of** *I dream of being a professional footballer.*
> **to set your heart on** *I have set my heart on being a professional footballer.*

> **6 9** OTHER WAYS OF SAYING *I want to be a professional footballer.*
> *My ambition is to be a professional footballer.*
> *My dream is to be a professional footballer.*

war *noun*

For three years, there was war between the two countries.
> ▶ **fighting   conflict**

warm *adjective*

1 *The soup was warm.*
> ▶ **lukewarm   tepid**

2 *It was a lovely warm day.*
> ▶ **hot   mild   sunny   boiling hot**

3 *We sat down in front of the warm fire.*
> ▶ **hot   blazing   roaring**

← → An opposite is **cold**.

warn *verb*

1 *He warned us to stay away from the old quarry.*
▶ to advise to remind to tell

2 *Someone had warned the police about the robbery.*
▶ to alert to tip someone off

3 *This time I will just warn you. If you do it again, you will be in big trouble.*
▶ to caution
to give someone a warning *This time I will just give you a warning.*

wash *verb*

1 *Go and wash your hands.*
▶ to clean to rinse

2 *You should wash more often.*
▶ to have a bath to bath to have a shower
to shower

3 *I washed my hair.*
▶ to shampoo

4 *I'm going to wash the floor.*
▶ to clean to mop to scrub to wipe

waste *noun*

Put the waste in the bin.
▶ rubbish litter junk refuse
trash (*American*)

watch *verb*

1 *I could feel that someone was watching me.*
▶ to look at to stare at to gaze at

2 *We sat and watched the badgers.*
▶ to observe

3 *Will you watch my things while I go for a swim?*
▶ to keep an eye on to look after to mind

a
b
c
d
e
f
g
h
i
j
k
l
m
n
o
p
q
r
s
t
u
v
w
x
y
z

water

water *noun*

 Focus on **water**

1 *Would you like a glass of water?*
▶ **mineral water   spring water   tap water**

2 *We sat by the side of the water.*
▶ **a lake   a pond   a reservoir   a river   a stream   the sea
the ocean   a brook**

SOME WORDS YOU MIGHT USE TO DESCRIBE HOW WATER
MOVES

to flow	**to trickle**	**to drip**
to pour	**to stream**	**to gush**
to splash	**to spray**	**to squirt**
to gurgle	**to lap**	

wave *verb*

1 *She waved to me from the other side of the field.*
▶ **to signal   to gesture**

2 *The flags were waving in the wind.*
▶ **to stir   to sway   to flap   to shake   to flutter**

3 *He waved the stick over his head.*
▶ **to swing   to brandish**

wave *noun*

We played in the waves.
▶ **a breaker** (*a big wave*)   **the surf**

way *noun*

1 *Is this the way to London?*
▶ **a road   a route**

2 *This is the best way to build a den.*
▶ **a method** *This is the best method of building a den.*
a technique *This is the best technique for building a den.*

3 *He spoke in a very angry way.*
▶ **a manner   a fashion**

4 *She ties her hair up in a very pretty way.*
▶ **a style**

a
b
c
d
e
f
g
h
i
j
k
l
m
n
o
p
q
r
s
t
u
v
w
x
y
z

weak *adjective*
1 *He is now very old and weak.*
   ▶ feeble frail shaky delicate
2 *She still feels quite weak after her illness.*
   ▶ ill poorly unwell
3 *You're too weak to fight against me!*
   ▶ weedy puny
4 *I think these wooden posts are too weak.*
   ▶ thin flimsy fragile
5 *This orange squash is too weak.*
   ▶ watery tasteless
← → An opposite is **strong**.

wealthy *adjective*
Her parents are wealthy.
   ▶ rich well-off prosperous
← → An opposite is **poor**.

weapon *noun*

••• SOME TYPES OF WEAPON		
a bomb	a bow and arrow	a cannon
a catapult	a cutlass	a dagger
a gun	a knife	a pistol
a revolver	a rifle	a sabre
a spear	a sword	

wear *verb*
1 *He was wearing a smart blue jacket.*
   ▶ to have on to be dressed in to be sporting
2 *What shall I wear today?*
   ▶ to put on to dress in

weather *noun*
What is the weather like in India?
   ▶ the climate

weird *adjective*
She wears some weird clothes!
▶ strange funny peculiar odd
←→ An opposite is **ordinary**.

welcome *verb*
We welcomed the guests at the door.
▶ to greet to receive

well *adjective*
I hope you are well.
▶ fit healthy
←→ An opposite is **ill**.

well *adverb*
1 *You have done this work very well.*
▶ carefully competently properly
←→ An opposite is **badly**.
2 *The concert went very well.*
▶ successfully
←→ An opposite is **badly**.
3 *Everyone in the team played well.*
▶ brilliantly excellently skilfully
←→ An opposite is **badly**.
4 *You explained that very well.*
▶ clearly
←→ An opposite is **badly**.
5 *They don't treat their pets very well.*
▶ kindly lovingly caringly
←→ An opposite is **badly**.
6 *Shake the bottle well before you open it.*
▶ thoroughly

well-known *adjective*
He's a very well-known pop star.
▶ famous celebrated
←→ An opposite is **unknown**.

a b c d e f g h i j k l m n o p q r s t u v w x y z

wet *adjective*
1 *My shoes are wet.*
▶ damp (*slightly wet*) soaked soaking wet
2 *I got wet in the rain.*
▶ soaked soaking wet dripping wet drenched
3 *The field is too wet to play on.*
▶ muddy soggy waterlogged
4 *It was a wet day.*
▶ rainy drizzly showery damp
← → An opposite is **dry**.

whisper *verb*
'Let's get out of here,' he whispered.
▶ to murmur to mutter to mumble to hiss

white *adjective*
She was wearing a white dress.
▶ cream ivory snow-white

whole *adjective*
We ate the whole cake.
▶ complete entire

wicked *adjective*
1 *The land was ruled by a wicked king.*
▶ bad evil
2 *That was a wicked thing to do.*
▶ wrong bad immoral sinful
← → An opposite is **good**.

wide *adjective*
We had to cross a wide river.
▶ broad big large
← → An opposite is **narrow**.

wild *adjective*
1 *They are wild animals and can be dangerous.*
▶ untamed ferocious
← → An opposite is **tame**.
2 *Their behaviour can be a bit wild sometimes.*
▶ noisy rough boisterous unruly
← → An opposite is **calm**.

will *verb*

1 *I will tell my teacher tomorrow.*
> ▶ **to intend to** *I intend to tell my teacher tomorrow.*

2 *I will help you.*
> ▶ **to be willing to** *I am willing to help you.*
> **to be happy to** *I am happy to help you.*

willing *adjective*
Are you willing to help us?
> ▶ **happy ready prepared**
> ← → An opposite is **unwilling**.

win *verb*

1 *I was delighted when my team won.*
> ▶ **to be victorious to triumph to come first**
> ← → An opposite is **lose**.

2 *She won a medal in the cross-country race.*
> ▶ **to get to earn to receive**

wind (*rhymes with* **tinned**) *noun*

🔍 *Focus on* **wind**

> *Outside, the wind was blowing.*
> ▶ **a breeze** (*a gentle wind*)
> **a gale** (*a strong wind*)
> **a hurricane** (*a very strong wind*)

SOME WORDS YOU MIGHT USE TO DESCRIBE HOW THE
WIND BLOWS
to blow   **to howl**   **to roar**
to whistle   **to buffet**

---

wind (*rhymes with* **find**) *verb*
She wound her scarf round her neck.
> ▶ **to wrap to loop to coil to twist**

windy *adjective*
It was a cold, windy night.
> ▶ **breezy blustery stormy**
> ← → An opposite is **calm**.

winner *noun*
James is the winner!
▶ the champion   the victor
←→ An opposite is **loser**.

wipe *verb*
1 *I'll wipe the table before we eat.*
▶ to clean
2 *She used a duster to wipe the furniture.*
▶ to dust   to polish
3 *Please could you wipe the mud off your shoes?*
▶ to rub   to scrape

wire *noun*
There were electrical wires all over the floor.
▶ a cable   a lead   a flex

wise *adjective*
1 *My grandfather is a very wise man.*
▶ clever   intelligent   sensible
2 *You have made a wise decision.*
▶ good   sensible
←→ An opposite is **foolish**.

wish for *verb*
I had always wished for a puppy.
▶ to want   to long for   to yearn for

witch *noun*
▶ a sorceress   an enchantress

wither *verb*
The plants withered because I forgot to water them.
▶ to dry up   to shrivel   to wilt

wizard *noun*
▶ a sorcerer   an enchanter   a magician

wobble *verb*
1 *The ladder wobbled as I climbed up it.*
▶ to shake   to sway   to be unsteady
2 *The jelly wobbles when you move the plate.*
▶ to shake   to quiver

a b c d e f g h i j k l m n o p q r s t u v w x y z

woman *noun*

What was the woman's name?
> ► a lady   a girl
> a mother (*a woman who has children*)
> a widow (*a woman whose husband has died*)

wonder *noun*

We stared at the lights in wonder.
> ► amazement   admiration   awe

wonder *verb*

I was wondering what to do next.
> ► to think about   to consider

wonderful *adjective*

We had a wonderful time.
> ► great   amazing   brilliant   fantastic   marvellous
>
> ← → An opposite is **terrible**.

wood *noun*

1 *Our garden shed is made of wood.*
> ► timber   planks

2 *We need more wood for the fire.*
> ► logs

3 *We walked through the wood.*
> ► woods   woodland   a forest   a copse (*a small wood*)

word *noun*

I can't think of the right word.
> ► a term   a phrase   an expression

work *noun*

1 *Just sit quietly and get on with your work.*
> ► a job   schoolwork   homework   a task

2 *What work do you want to do when you grow up?*
> ► a job   an occupation   a profession   a career

3 *The work can be back-breaking.*
> ► labour   toil

w

work *verb*
 1 *We worked hard all morning.*
  ▶ **to be busy** *We were busy all morning.*
    to toil *We toiled all morning.*
 2 *When I grow up I want to work in a bank.*
  ▶ **to be employed   to have a job**
 3 *The lift isn't working.*
  ▶ **to go** *The lift doesn't go.*
    to function *The lift isn't functioning.*
 4 *I don't think your plan will work.*
  ▶ **to succeed   to be successful**

worried *adjective*
 1 *I was worried because they were so late home.*
  ▶ **anxious   concerned**
 2 *Are you worried about moving to a new school?*
  ▶ **nervous   apprehensive**
 ← → An opposite is **relaxed**.

worry *verb*
 Don't worry, everything will be all right.
  ▶ **to fret   to be anxious   to be concerned**

worry *noun*
 I seem to have so many worries at the moment.
  ▶ **a concern   a fear**

wound *noun*
 He had a nasty wound on his arm.
  ▶ **an injury   a cut   a gash**

wound *verb*
 The explosion wounded a lot of people.
  ▶ **to injure   to hurt**

wrap *verb*
 1 *I wrapped the parcel in paper.*
  ▶ **to cover   to pack**
 2 *I wrapped my scarf round my neck.*
  ▶ **to wind   to loop**

a

b

c

d

e

f

g

h

i

j

k

l

m

n

o

p

q

r

s

t

u

v

w

x

y

z

wreck *verb*

1 *The explosion wrecked several buildings.*
  ▸ **to destroy** **to demolish** **to smash up**

2 *He drove into a lamppost and wrecked his car.*
  ▸ **to smash up**

3 *You've wrecked my CD player!*
  ▸ **to break** **to ruin** **to smash**

write *verb*

1 *He wrote the word 'birthday' at the top of the page.*
  ▸ **to print** (*to write without the letters joined up*)
    to jot down (*to write quickly*)
    to scribble (*to write messily*)
    to scrawl (*to write very messily*)

2 *Please write your name here.*
  ▸ **to sign**

3 *I wrote a list of all the things we would need.*
  ▸ **to compile** **to make**

4 *Sometimes we write stories at school.*
  ▸ **to make up**

5 *We're going to write a piece of music.*
  ▸ **to compose** **to create**

writer *noun*

I want to be a writer when I grow up.
  ▸ **an author**

> ••• SOME TYPES OF WRITER
>   **a journalist** (*someone who writes for a newspaper*)
>   **a novelist**
>   **a playwright** (*someone who writes plays*)
>   **a poet**
>   **a scriptwriter** (*someone who writes scripts for films*)

wrong *adjective*

1 *The information that he gave us was wrong.*
  ▸ **false** **inaccurate** **untrue** **incorrect**

2 *I thought she lived here, but I was wrong.*
  ▸ **mistaken**

3 *It is wrong to steal.*
  ▸ **dishonest** **immoral** **bad** **wicked**

  ← → An opposite is **right**.

yell *verb*
The man yelled at us to go away.
► to shout to scream to shriek to bawl to bellow

yellow *adjective*
The bridesmaids wore yellow dresses.
► lemon gold primrose

young *adjective*
1 *I was too young to understand what was happening.*
► little small
←→ An opposite is **old**.
2 *She seems a bit young for her age.*
► immature childish
←→ An opposite is **mature**.
3 *My dad is forty, but he still looks quite young.*
► youthful
←→ An opposite is **old**.

a
b
c
d
e
f
g
h
i
j
k
l
m
n
o
p
q
r
s
t
u
v
w
x
y
z

Zz

zap *verb*

I've got a new computer game in which you have to zap aliens.
▶ to kill   to shoot   to destroy   to blast   to hit

zero *noun*

1 *The temperature went down to zero.*
▶ nought   nothing

2 *The other team won by three goals to zero.*
▶ nil

zoom *verb*

The car zoomed along the motorway.
▶ to speed   to race   to tear   to hurtle

Help with punctuation

These are the punctuation marks that will make your writing easier to understand:

apostrophe	**,**	Use an apostrophe to show that a letter has been left out of a word for example, *don't*, or to show belonging, for example, *the cat's tail*.
brackets	**( )**	You use brackets around things that are interesting but not necessary, for example, *the cat's tail (which was black and very long) was caught in the door.*
colon	**:**	You use a colon when you have a list of things coming after a heading. You also use a colon in a sentence when you have examples to list, for example, *I got a lot of birthday presents: a camera, a chess set, a skateboard, a jacket and an ink pen*. A colon is also used when you have two sentences and the second sentence explains what is meant in the first, for example, *the cat is in trouble again: it is stuck in the tree.*
comma	**,**	You use a comma to show a small break in a sentence.
dash	**–**	Dashes are useful to show an interruption or bigger break in a sentence.
exclamation mark	**!**	An exclamation mark shows surprise or urgency.
full stop	**.**	A full stop is used at the end of a sentence.
hyphen	**–**	A hyphen joins words or parts of words together, for example, hard-boiled.
question mark	**?**	A question mark shows a question is being asked.
semi-colon	**;**	You use a semi-colon to show more of a break than a comma.
speech marks	**' '**	You use these to around the words that a person speaks, for example, *'You are in the team,' said Miss Johnson.*

Word classes (parts of speech)

There are eight word classes, or parts of speech:

Adjective	An **adjective** is a word which describes a noun and tells you what something is like, for example how big it is, how old it is, what colour it is, what it looks like and feels like. In the phrase, *a big, colourful rainbow*, *big* and *colourful* are adjectives. Many adjectives can be used to compare things - they have two forms: **comparative** and **superlative.** You use the comparative form such as *bigger* or *smaller* and superlative form such as *biggest* or *smallest* to compare different things. The comparative and superlative form is often made by adding *-er* and *-est* to the adjective. This does not work for some adjectives such as *dangerous*. To create the comparative form you would need to use *more colourful* or *most colourful*.
Adverb	An **adverb** is a word which tells you how, when, or where something happens. Some adverbs tell you how someone does something, for example *quickly, slowly, carefully* and *lazily*.
Conjunction	A **conjunction** is a word which joins words or ideas. *And* or *but* are conjunctions.
Interjection or exclamation	Words like *Hello!* or *Well!* are **exclamations.**
Noun	A **noun** is the name of a person, thing or idea. *House* and *gift* are nouns.
	Proper nouns are the names of particular places, persons or things. Nouns can be **countable**, for example, *girl* and *car*. You can say *three girls* and *four cars*. They can also be **uncountable**, for example, *grass* or *butter*. You cannot say *two grasses* or *three butters*.
	Abstract nouns are those things that you can't see or touch such as *air, happiness* or *luck*.

	Collective nouns are words for groups or sets of things e.g. a *herd* of cattle, a *flock* of sheep.
	Plural nouns are nouns that do not have a singular form e.g. *trousers*.
Preposition	**Prepositions** are words that give information on the position of things e.g. *on, under, behind, at*. In the phrases, *across the drive*, or *under the car*, *across* and *under* are prepositions.
Pronoun	A **pronoun** is a word which you use instead of a noun. For example, instead of saying *The dog ran away*, you can say *It ran away*, and instead of saying *I like my teacher*, you san say *I like he.r*
	Personal pronouns are *you, me, I, he, him, she, her, it*. The plurals of these personal pronouns are *you, we, us, you, they, them*.
	Possessive pronouns show who something belongs to e.g. *my, your, his, her, its, our, their* and *mine, yours, hers, ours, theirs*. Other pronouns such as *who, what, some, which* and *whose* are for asking questions.
Verb	A **verb** is a doing word which shows what someone does or what happens. In the sentence *Jo ran home*, and *the rain stopped*, *ran* and *stopped* are verbs.

Using prefixes

prefix	meaning	examples
aero-	to do with air or aircraft	*aerobatics*
anti-	against or opposite	*antifreeze.* If the word you are adding *anti-* to begins with a vowel, you use a hyphen, e.g. *anti-aircraft*
audio-	to do with sound or hearing	*audio-visual*
auto-	self	*autobiography, automatic*
bi-	two	*bicycle, bilateral*
bio-	life	*biology, biography*
co-	together with someone else	*co-pilot, co-author, cooperate, coordinate*
counter-	opposite	*counterproductive, counter-claim, counterbalance*
cross-	across	*crossroads, crosswinds, cross-curricular*
de-	to take something away	*debug, de-ice, defrost*
dis-	opposite	*dislike, disagree, disobey*
e-	electronic	*email, e-shopping*
ex-	in the past	*ex-policeman, ex-president*
geo-	earth	*geography, geology*
in- (also im-)	opposite, not	*incorrect, insane, impossible, impolite*
micro-	small	*microchip, micro-organism*
mid-	in the middle	*midday, midnight, midsummer*
mini-	very small	*minibus, miniskirt*
mis-	badly or wrongly	*misbehave, misspell*
multi-	many	*multicoloured, multicultural*
non-	not	*non-existent, non-fiction, non-stop*

over-	too much	*overactive, oversleep*
photo-	light	*photocopy, photograph*
pre-	before	*prefabricated, pre-school*
re-	again	*rebuild, re-cover, re-enter, reheat*
semi-	half	*semicircle, semi-final, semi-detached*
sub-	under	*submarine, subway*
super-	bigger or very good	*super-hero, superhuman, supermodel*
un-	opposite, not	*unable, uncomfortable, unhappy*

Using suffixes

for making nouns

-hood	*child-childhood, father-fatherhood*
-ity	*stupid-stupidity, pure-purity*
-ness	*happy-happiness, kind-kindness*
-ment	*enjoy-enjoyment, move-movement*
-ship	*friend-friendship, champion-championship*
-sion	*divide-division, persuade-persuasion*
-tion	*subtract-subtraction, react-reaction*

for making adjectives

-able	*enjoy-enjoyable, forgive-forgivable*
-ful	*hope-hopeful, colour-colourful*
-ible	*eat-edible, reverse-reversible*
-ic	*allergy-allergic, science-scientific*
-ish	*child-childish*
-ive	*explode-explosive*
-less	*fear-fearless, hope-hopeless*
-like	*life-lifelike*
-y	*anger-angry, hair-hairy*

for making nouns that mean a person who does something

-er, -or	*act-actor, paint-painter*

-ist   *science-scientist, art-artist*

for making feminine nouns

-ess   *actor-actress, lion-lioness*

for making adverbs

-ly   *careful-carefully, quick-quickly*

for making verbs

-ate   *active-activate, pollen-pollinate*

-en   *damp-dampen, short-shorten*

-ify   *solid-solidify, liquid-liquify*

-ize, -ise *apology-apologize, fossil-fossilize*